COLLINS CLASSICS

The Strange Case of Dr Jekyll and Mr Hyde

by

Robert Louis Stevenson

Adapted by
Simon Adorian

Resource Material by
Sue Cottam

Series Consultant
Stephen Cockett

Ideas for the resource pages were developed in workshops during
Autumn 1997 with students of St Osmund's Middle School, Dorchester,
Dorset. The script was first staged at the school in July 1998.

Collins Educational

Published by Collins Educational,
An imprint of HarperCollins*Publishers* Ltd,
77–85 Fulham Palace Road, London W6 8JB

© 1999 playscript Simon Adorian, resource material Sue Cottam

First published 1999

ISBN 000 323 078 3

Simon Adorian asserts the moral right to be identified as the author of the playscript; Sue Cottam asserts the moral right to be identified as the author of the resource material.

British Library Cataloguing in Publication Data
A catalogue record for this book is available from the British Library.

Commissioned by Helen Clark, edited by Katie Taylor and Toby Satterthwaite, picture research by Catherine Dey

Design by Nigel Jordan, cover design by Nigel Jordan, cover illustration by Alan Marks

Acknowledgements
The following permissions to reproduce material are gratefully acknowledged:
Illustrations: Nigel Jordan, pp. 54-55; Topham Picturepoint, pp. 58, 68: Museum of London, p. 70; The Illustrated London News Picture Library, p. 72; Simon Morgan, pp. 75, 79; Birmingham City Council, Central Library, p. 82; photographs by permission of the Metropolitan Police Service, pp. 85, 86.
Text extracts: Peters, Fraser and Dunlop, p. 78; St Martin's Press, p. 86; adapted from the Dorset Evening Echo, p. 90; The Guardian, p. 91, 92, 93; The Independent and Jeremy Laurance, p. 94.

Production by Susan Cashin, printed and bound in Hong Kong

For permission to perform this play, please allow plenty of time and contact:
Permissions Department, HarperCollins*Publishers*,
77–85 Fulham Palace Road, London W6 8JB. Tel. 0181 741 7070.

Contents

Setting

A present-day TV studio with live audience, presenter and panel of experts.

Re-enactments of the past by studio actors and actresses in Victorian streets of London and gentlemen's London residences.

KEY

71–74
71–74▶   cross-reference between playscript and teaching resources.

H   in resources = activity suitable for homework.

Characters

LONDON, 1882–1884

DR HENRY JEKYLL a well-known doctor

MR EDWARD HYDE a mysterious associate of Dr Jekyll

POOLE Jekyll's manservant

HASTIE LANYON doctor and friend of Jekyll

LANYON'S HOUSEKEEPER

MR GABRIEL UTTERSON a lawyer and friend of Jekyll

MR RICHARD ENFIELD a young man about town

ELLEN CROSS a maidservant

INSPECTOR NEWCOMEN from Scotland Yard

SIR DANVERS CAREW MP

DAISY a young girl

DAISY'S MOTHER

NEIGHBOURS

DOCTOR

NEWS BOYS

CHORUS – the voices inside Jekyll's head. At times the chorus divides into two parts, **C1** and **C2**. These may represent good and evil, though you can experiment with other ways of dividing up their lines.

A TV STUDIO, LONDON, PRESENT DAY

DIRECTOR

PRESENTER

ROSALYN CROFT a historian

DR JUDE FALLON a psychologist

LAWRENCE BENNETT a retired police inspector

PAULINE HILL a graphologist

PRODUCTION ASSISTANTS AND TECHNICIANS

The Strange Case of
Dr Jekyll and Mr Hyde

ACT ONE

*Before the play begins, we see a television studio set. People with clipboards walk the floor and check lights, props etc. If possible, there are cameras linked to a couple of monitors. Someone is on a ladder putting the last touches to a sign that reads 'Strange Cases'. A panel of smartly dressed experts sit at a table with their names on display: **Croft**, **Fallon**, **Bennett**. They look at their papers and are making last-minute notes. Opposite the panel stands an empty courtroom dock.*

*A **Presenter** sits apart on a separate chair. In another area is a group of actors in Victorian costumes. Some of them are calling for make-up assistants who apply the final touches.*

Scene One

DIRECTOR Clear the set. Cue music and credits. And … action.

*Mood-setting music. If there are cameras, they focus on the 'Strange Cases' sign and we see it on the monitors. The **Presenter** stands and talks to camera.*

PRESENTER Welcome to a new series of 'Strange Cases', in which we put notorious unsolved mysteries of the past under the spotlight. Our panel of experts in law, science and criminology re-examine cases that have, up till now, baffled investigators and defied the law.

Tonight's mystery is no exception. It takes us into the foggy backstreets of Victorian London to reveal an unprovoked assault on a child, the motiveless murder of a leading politician, the disappearance of a well-known doctor and the suicide of a sinister stranger. As well as these chilling events, we shall learn about a disturbing experiment in drugs – so disturbing that its only witness died from shock.

As ever, our cast of actors will present studio reconstructions of key incidents in the case and, drawing on all the surviving evidence and documents, they will take on the roles of the principal figures for interrogation from our panel.

Tonight's episode is not for the faint-hearted: it offers us a haunting insight into the dark side of human nature and paranormal experience. We bring you 'The Strange Case of Dr Jekyll and Mr Hyde.'

Music.

PRESENTER Our story opens with the evidence of a Mr Richard Enfield, a well-known young man about town, who, in the winter of 1882, found himself witness to a bizarre assault in a London back street. He gave an account of the incident to his lawyer. Even today it makes shocking reading.

Enfield *enters the dock. As he gives his evidence, the actors take up position ready to perform the scene.*

PRESENTER Mr Enfield, can you please set the scene for us?

ENFIELD I was coming home from a party, from some place at the end of the world, about three o'clock of a black winter morning, and my way brought me through a part of town where there was literally nothing to be seen but lamps. Street after street, and all the folks asleep – street after street, all lighted up as if for a procession, and all as empty as a church. At last I got into that state of mind when a man listens and listens … and begins to long for the sight of a policeman. And then I saw two figures. One, a little man who was stumping along at a cracking pace, the other a girl of maybe eight or ten who was –

PRESENTER Let me stop you there, Mr Enfield. An eight-year-old girl? Out on her own at three o'clock in the morning? Hardly a normal occurrence, I should have thought.

ENFIELD My own thoughts entirely. It turned out later that she had been sent by her family for the doctor. It was an emergency and the child was running as hard as she was able down a cross-street.

Scene Two

*The actors – **Daisy** and **Hyde** – now take over the action in the main stage space. **Enfield** comes out from the dock and looks on. **Daisy** and **Hyde** run and collide at a street corner. **Daisy** falls back and screams out in terror. **Hyde** takes a step back and looks coldly at her. Then he calmly and deliberately tramples over her, leaving her screaming in the street. **Hyde** walks away and **Enfield** pursues him.*

ENFIELD Hey! Stop! You sir! Come back at once!

*Enfield sets off after **Hyde**, shouting as he goes. As he does so, a small crowd gathers in the street. Most are wearing night-clothes. **Daisy's Mother** and **Neighbours** appear and try to calm her, as she is still crying and screaming.*

DAISY *(crying)* He did it on purpose... He... he... stamped me. He trampled me. Oh, Mum... did you see his face? Did you see his evil face?

MOTHER It's all right, love. You're all right.

DAISY But he... he... just... just didn't care.

NEIGHBOUR 1 Must be a madman. Attacking a little child like that.

NEIGHBOUR 2 Drunk more like. We'll soon have him if he dare come back this way.

MOTHER Here comes the doctor now, love.

*Enter the **Doctor** who starts to examine **Daisy**. **Enfield** returns, holding **Hyde** by the neck. Despite the anger of the crowd, **Hyde** remains cold and calm throughout this scene.*

HYDE Take your hand off my collar. Thank you.

ENFIELD I've a good mind to take a whip to you, sir. How dare you attack an innocent child who has no one with her to protect her? It sounds like nothing much but, I tell you all, it was hellish to see. He just trampled over her. It wasn't like a man; it was like some damned juggernaut!

NEIGHBOUR 1 I know what I'd do to him. String him up from that post.

Neighbour 2 Yeah, leave 'im to us, mate. We'll see to 'im.

*The crowd are really angry now and start to close in. **Hyde** stands his ground and they back off.*

Hyde Stop your bleating, the pack of you. You think I honestly care? The child is barely injured – ask your friend the sawbones here. Am I right?

Doctor Well, more frightened than injured, I should say. But I hardly think that's the point.

Enfield Frankly, sir, you disgust me.

The crowd murmurs its approval.

Neighbour 1 Hanging's too good for the likes of you.

Hyde I hardly think that a minor collision with some… street urchin is likely to be a capital offence. You people and your wretched whining are beginning to tire me. Time you were in your beds.

Doctor How dare you talk to these good folk like that?

Hyde It's all they understand.

*Some of the crowd are now very angry. Two women try to get hold of **Hyde** and have to be restrained by **Enfield** and the **Doctor**.*

Mother He called my Daisy a street urchin. I'll kill 'im.

Enfield Ladies, please. Sadly, killing is out of the question. But we can do the next best thing. *(to **Hyde**)* Don't think this will end here. We'll make such a scandal out of this as will make your name stink from one end of London to the other.

Hyde Huh!

Enfield You may well sneer, sir, but I promise you that if you have any friends or credit in this town –

Doctor Unlikely…

ENFIELD – you shall lose them.

HYDE So that's what it comes to. Blackmail. Well, I do not want a scene. Name your figure.

ENFIELD I should say fifty pounds would be the least you could do to make amends to this girl and her family.

The crowd is impressed. They whisper 'fifty pounds' to one another. **Hyde** *looks slowly at the angry crowd.*

HYDE Let's call it a hundred. *(Shocked reaction from the crowd.)* You'll take a cheque, I presume?

He turns and walks off. **Enfield** *goes with him, but returns to the dock. The other characters exit quietly and we return to the* **Presenter** *who continues to quiz* **Enfield***.*

Scene Three

PRESENTER And he paid you in full, Mr Enfield?

ENFIELD He did. Ten pounds in cash, the rest a cheque. But …

PRESENTER Yes?

ENFIELD He led myself and the doctor to a house. In a courtyard, not two streets away. Two storeys high, no windows, nothing but a door – a door with no bell or knocker. I had never seen a house so sinister and so neglected. The man went inside and presently reappeared with the cash and a cheque for the balance. But the cheque was made out in another man's name.

PRESENTER May we ask, whose name?

ENFIELD The cheque was signed by one Dr Henry Jekyll. I had never met him, but he was a highly respectable man, well known for his charities and his religion – what you might call a do-gooder.

PRESENTER An unlikely sponsor for this Mr Hyde, don't you think?

Enfield I was suspicious. After all, in real life, a man does not walk into a cellar door at four in the morning and come out of it with another man's cheque for close upon a hundred pounds. We were wise to this game and marched him off to my chambers where we spent the night guarding him until the banks were open next morning. After we had breakfasted we went in a body to the bank. I gave in the cheque myself and said I had every reason to believe it was a forgery. Not a bit of it. The cheque was genuine.

Presenter Thank you, Mr Enfield. We would now like to involve the panel in our investigations. *(to Croft)* First of all, Rosalyn Croft, you're a historian with a particular interest in Victorian social conditions. A child assaulted in the street by a complete stranger – can you really believe that this could happen?

Croft Oh yes, I find the story quite feasible. In many parts of London, incidents of violence and mayhem were far more common than they would be nowadays. We know that they didn't always come to official notice, but we also know that they happened.

Presenter An assault on a child – and no legal action?

Croft But our friend, Mr Enfield here, has told us that he helped the family to obtain damages. Very generous damages. A hundred pounds then would have been a year's wages for a working man. To be honest, this was a better result than they would have got through the courts. This crowd was prepared to be bought off. People in the slums of Victorian London – like the people in the slums of any city at any time – needed to look after themselves because the authorities wouldn't do it.

Presenter Thank you. *(now addressing last member of panel)* Dr Jude Fallon, you're a psychologist with experience in cases of violent crime. Any questions?

Fallon Yes. Mr Enfield...

Enfield Ma'am.

Fallon I'd like to concentrate on our man who attacked this child. One obvious question: did he give you a name?

ENFIELD He said his name was Hyde.

FALLON You have not told us anything about what he was like. Can you describe him?

ENFIELD Not easily. There was... something wrong with his appearance.

FALLON Something wrong?

ENFIELD He seemed... deformed ...

FALLON Ah ha! So we have a distinguishing characteristic! Describe it.

ENFIELD That's just the point. I am unable to. There was something so hateful, so... An extraordinary-looking man and yet I can give you nothing out of the way. It's not for want of memory, for I can see him this minute. A face which haunts me, a face utterly without mercy. If you saw that face, madam, you would hate it too. *(shudders and hides his own face before recovering his composure)* I'm sorry.

FALLON It's all right, Mr Enfield. I can believe that the experience was an upsetting one. I have no more questions.

PRESENTER And now our final member of the panel, Lawrence Bennett, a retired police inspector.

BENNETT Mr Enfield. I'd like to ask you about the house which this Mr Hyde took you to. You say it had no bell or knocker.

ENFIELD Correct.

BENNETT So how did he gain access?

ENFIELD With a key. I distinctly remember that he let himself in.

BENNETT And do you have any idea whose house this was?

ENFIELD I do not.

BENNETT And you didn't try to find out who lived there?

ENFIELD No, sir, I did not. It is a rule of mine not to ask too many questions. You never know where it might lead you.

BENNETT Quite. One final point, Mr Enfield.

ENFIELD Mmm?

BENNETT Did you tell this story to anyone?

ENFIELD I told it to one man only. A friend of mine, a distant relative, and a lawyer besides. Someone I knew I could trust to keep it to himself.

BENNETT His name?

ENFIELD Utterson. Mr Gabriel Utterson.

*Enfield extends a welcoming gesture towards **Utterson** who now moves towards the dock.*

PRESENTER *(to camera)* Any investigation of this case leads us quickly to Mr Gabriel Utterson, the lawyer friend of both Mr Enfield and the highly respected Dr Henry Jekyll.

Utterson now stands in the dock.

PRESENTER Mr Utterson, may I ask you if you were in any way surprised by the story you were told by Enfield?

UTTERSON Not surprised. But it did confirm some of my worst fears.

PRESENTER Fears for whom?

UTTERSON For my friend Jekyll. At the time I could share this with no one, but I had in my possession this document which had to remain confidential. *(takes out the will)* It was the will of my friend Harry Jekyll and, as his lawyer, I had taken charge of it.

BENNETT Presumably, if you acted as his lawyer, you had helped to draw it up.

UTTERSON Absolutely not! I refused to have anything to do with it. The whole business offended me.

BENNETT Can you share the will with us? Without too much detail, of course.

UTTERSON Oh, it's not a complicated document. That's not the problem. The main provision is quite straightforward... here it is... *(reading from the will)* 'that in the case of the decease of Dr Henry Jekyll, M.D., D.C.L., F.R.S. etc., all his possessions are to pass into the hands of his friend and benefactor Edward Hyde.'

CROFT But is that really so strange? After all there could be many reasons for Jekyll leaving his money to that man.

UTTERSON That is not the part that troubled me. Here we are. It contains another clause. *(reading again)* 'That in the case of Dr Jekyll's disappearance or unexplained absence for any period exceeding three calendar months the said Mr Hyde shall step into the said Henry Jekyll's shoes without further delay.'

FALLON 'Disappearance or unexplained absence'?

UTTERSON Those are the terms of the will.

FALLON And what do you think the doctor meant by this?

UTTERSON I can only say what it meant to me. It offended me as a lawyer – and as a sensible man. I thought it was madness. But once I had heard Enfield's story, I began to fear it was disgrace.

PRESENTER *(to Croft)* Rosalyn Croft, historian. You hinted earlier that there were explanations for an apparent stranger being left money in a rich man's will.

CROFT Absolutely. As Utterson himself said, this seems to point towards some past disgrace in Jekyll's life. Perhaps Hyde was blackmailing the older man. There's another possible relationship between Jekyll and Hyde. Many respectable Victorian gentlemen had illegitimate children who they could not own up to in society but who they still wanted to look after. But that bit about disappearance or ... what was the phrase again?

UTTERSON 'Unexplained absence ... '

CROFT That is most odd.

PRESENTER *(to Fallon)* Jude Fallon – as a psychologist, do you have any thoughts on that?

FALLON Just that it is such a strange clause to put in a will. It suggests Henry Jekyll had some reason for accepting the possibility of an 'unexplained absence'. Mr Utterson, had the doctor ever gone missing before?

UTTERSON Not that I was aware.

FALLON Was there anyone else who knew him as well as you did?

UTTERSON Just one man. Dr Hastie Lanyon. He, Harry and myself had been old mates both at school and college. It was obvious that I should sound him out on this matter – if anyone knew, it would be Lanyon.

Music as the actors move into a reconstruction. **Utterson** *leaves the dock and puts on his coat. He moves across the stage where he is welcomed by a* **Housekeeper**.

Scene Four

UTTERSON Is Dr Lanyon at home?

HOUSEKEEPER This way, sir. The doctor is in the dining room, but he will see you at once.

Lanyon is sitting at a table. There is a bottle of wine and a glass on the table. As soon as **Utterson** *approaches,* **Lanyon** *jumps to his feet.*

LANYON Utterson! Good man! You will join me, won't you?

UTTERSON Hastie, I cannot stay long. I need to talk to you about a confidential matter that has been troubling me for some time.

LANYON If I can help in any way…

UTTERSON It is about Henry Jekyll. I suppose you and I must be the oldest friends he has.

LANYON I wish the friends were younger. *(laughs)* But yes, I suppose we are. And what of it? I see little of him now.

UTTERSON Indeed? But I thought you had so much in common.

LANYON We had. We were the closest of colleagues, but he began to go wrong, wrong in the mind. I still take an interest in him for old time's sake, as they say, but I see devilish little of the man.

These experiments and theories of his – they're just claptrap, scientific balderdash!

UTTERSON I'm sorry to hear of your differences. But, tell me, did you ever come across a protégé of his – one Hyde?

LANYON Hyde? No. Never heard of him. Since my time.

Scene Five

Lights fade on this scene as **Utterson** *walks towards the dock and takes up the story once more.*

UTTERSON Lanyon could not help me, but still I continued to dig away at the problem. The idea of this man Hyde began to enslave my imagination. At night it even haunted my dreams, gliding stealthily through sleeping streets where at every corner it would crush a child and leave it screaming. But it was always a figure without a face and I became overcome with a curious obsession to set eyes on the features of the real Mr Hyde. I stalked the streets around Jekyll's house, day and night, in the hope of catching a glimpse of this man. If he be Mr Hyde, I thought, I shall be Mr Seek. And at last, late one dry, frosty night, my patience was rewarded.

Scene Six

Lights change. Night-time. We hear **Hyde's** *footsteps and he enters furtively. He looks around him and, approaching a door, he takes a key from his pocket.* **Utterson** *steps out and touches* **Hyde** *on the shoulder.* **Hyde** *shrinks back, hissing. He turns away so that his face is in shadow.*

UTTERSON Mr Hyde, I think?

HYDE *(cold and calm)* That is my name. What do you want?

UTTERSON I see you are going in here. I am an old friend of Dr Jekyll's – Mr Utterson of Gaunt Street – you must have heard my name. Will you let me in?

HYDE You will not find Dr Jekyll. He is from home. How did you know me?

UTTERSON On your side, will you do me a favour?

HYDE What shall it be?

UTTERSON Will you let me see your face?

*Hyde hesitates, then turns to face **Utterson**. They stare at one another for a few seconds.*

UTTERSON Now I shall know you again. It may be useful.

HYDE Yes, useful. I may have need of you one day. You should have my address. *(**Hyde** gives a card to **Utterson**)* And now, how did you know me?

UTTERSON By description.

HYDE Whose?

UTTERSON We have common friends.

HYDE Common friends! Who are they?

UTTERSON Jekyll, for instance.

HYDE *(angrily)* He never told you. You're a liar!

*Hyde turns the key and disappears into the house. **Utterson** returns to the dock. Lights on studio area.*

Scene Seven

PRESENTER Once you had met this Mr Hyde, did you feel any easier in your mind?

UTTERSON I did not. For a start, the door to which he held the key was one I already recognised. It was the door to the outbuildings of a much larger house fronting another street. It led to the laboratory at the back of the house belonging to... Dr Henry Jekyll.

FALLON Tell me, Mr Utterson, was this your first meeting with Mr Hyde?

UTTERSON It turned out to be the only time I ever saw him alive. Yet he filled me with fear, loathing and disgust. The man seemed hardly human. If ever I read Satan's signature upon a face, it was on that of Jekyll's new friend.

FALLON But he didn't try to avoid you. He even gave you his address. Any idea why?

UTTERSON I guessed he was thinking of the will and knew I was the lawyer. I feared he was anxious to inherit and... planning to kill Jekyll.

BENNETT Forgive me for asking such an obvious question, Mr Utterson, but why didn't you discuss this with Dr Jekyll himself?

UTTERSON That was my next move.

Scene Eight

Lights on central acting area, which now becomes Dr Jekyll's house.
***Utterson** is being admitted by Jekyll's manservant, **Poole**.*

POOLE Good evening, Mr Utterson. Allow me to take your coat, sir.

UTTERSON Thank you, Poole.

POOLE Dr Jekyll is expecting you. I will inform him that you have arrived.

***Poole** turns to go, but **Utterson** calls him back.*

UTTERSON Poole?

POOLE Sir?

UTTERSON Before you go through, there's something I should like to ask you. The other night I met a certain Mr Hyde going in by the laboratory door at the back of the house. He quite clearly told me that Dr Jekyll was not at home. Is that right?

POOLE Quite right, Mr Utterson, sir. Mr Hyde has a key.

UTTERSON Your master seems to place a great deal of trust in that young man, Poole.

POOLE Yes, sir, he does indeed. We all have orders to obey Mr Hyde.

UTTERSON I don't think I have ever met him in the house?

POOLE Oh dear no, sir. He never dines here. Indeed, we see very little of him on this side of the house. He mostly comes and goes by the laboratory. I will inform Dr Jekyll that you are here.

*Poole leaves. **Utterson** paces the room and mutters to himself.*

UTTERSON See little of him... orders to obey him... comes and goes by the laboratory door. I don't like this. Poor Harry Jekyll, I fear he is in deep water.

*Jekyll comes through. He gives **Utterson** a bluff welcome, calling out his name and shaking his hand warmly.*

JEKYLL Utterson! How are you, old chap?

UTTERSON Harry!

JEKYLL Come, take a seat. Why don't you stay and dine with me? I am alone tonight.

UTTERSON I am sorry. I am in a hurry.

JEKYLL A hurry, eh? Well, how can I help you?

UTTERSON I have been wanting to speak to you, Jekyll. You know that will of yours?

JEKYLL I would rather not discuss that. I thought we had agreed.

UTTERSON You know I have never approved of it.

JEKYLL *(laughing at him)* If it's not you disapproving of my business, it's that old pedant Lanyon complaining about my scientific research. At this rate I shall become an outcast.

UTTERSON This is no joking matter. And I have been learning something of young Hyde.

Jekyll reacts sharply.

JEKYLL I don't care to hear any more. I thought we had agreed to drop this matter.

UTTERSON What I heard was abominable.

JEKYLL It can make no difference to the will. You don't understand my situation – it's a strange one, a very strange one. It is one of those things that can't be mended by talking.

UTTERSON Jekyll, you know me. You can trust me. Make a clean breast of this in confidence and I am certain I can get you out of it.

JEKYLL My good Utterson, this is downright good of you, and I cannot find the words to thank you. I believe you fully. I would trust you before any man alive, but indeed it isn't what you fear. It's not so bad as that.

UTTERSON I am relieved to hear it.

JEKYLL Just to put your good heart at rest, I'll tell you one thing. The moment I choose, I can be rid of Mr Hyde. I give you my word on that. I thank you again, but this is a private matter, and I beg of you to let it sleep.

UTTERSON *(after a pause)* Perhaps you are right.

JEKYLL I really have a great interest in poor Hyde. I know you have met him – he told me so – and I fear he was rude. But I do take a very great interest in that young man. And if I am taken away, I want you to promise that you will bear with him and get his rights for him. I think you would, if you knew everything.

UTTERSON I can't promise that I shall ever like him.

JEKYLL I don't ask that. I only ask for justice. I only ask you to help him for my sake, when I am no longer here.

UTTERSON Well. I promise.

Lights fade to blackout.

Scene Nine

Music. As the lights come up and the music plays we hear the voices of **News Boys***.*

NEWS BOYS Read all about it!
  Special edition!
  Shocking murder of MP!
  Midnight horror!
  Read all about it!

*Lights on **Presenter** in studio area.*

PRESENTER *(to camera)* Nearly a year later, in October 1883, London was rocked by the news of a crime of shocking ferocity. There was only one witness, a young maidservant, Ellen Cross, who provided the police with a graphic account. She gave her evidence to Inspector Newcomen of Scotland Yard.

*Spotlight on **Cross** who stands in the dock area. **Newcomen** stands opposite her.*

CROSS I was lookin' out the window in my attic room, lookin' out across the Embankment. It was a full moon and I suppose I was just kind of dreaming, you know, looking at the fog coming off the river, like. And this old feller comes along, a really nice old feller –

NEWCOMEN Miss Cross, how could you tell whether or not he was 'a nice old fellow' from your third-floor window?

CROSS Well, 'e just looked it. You know 'ow it is, sometimes you can just kind of sense it. A nice-looking old man, with long silvery hair, a gentleman. And then this other little man, a younger man, he comes down the lane in a real dash. And the old fellow, he sort of bows, all polite like, and raises his hat and says something.

NEWCOMEN Did you hear what he said?

CROSS Oh no, sir, I was too far away to 'ear what they was saying. But you could tell it was just something friendly like. I fancied 'e might've asked 'im the way or the time or something. Anyway, then this Mr Hyde –

NEWCOMEN Mr Hyde. You mean you recognised the younger man?

CROSS Oh yes, sir. He came to my master's once and I recognised 'im for sure. You don't forget a face like 'is in an 'urry, I can tell yer.

NEWCOMEN So tell me exactly what you saw.

CROSS Well, as I said, this Mr Hyde, 'e 'as this big, heavy walking cane, right, and 'e's kind of playing with it but in a real evil way if you get my drift and staring at the old boy and looking right angry. And the old feller, 'e's backin' off and I could tell as 'e was scared and 'e looked all helpless. And then... *(starts to sob)*

NEWCOMEN Please, Miss Cross, this is very important. Try to tell everything.

CROSS Then Hyde just snaps. Breaks out in anger, stamps 'is foot, swinging 'is cane and carryin' on like some sort of madman. And 'e starts clubbin' the old chap, really clubbin' 'im 'ard, like a ape. And next thing 'e's on 'im like a trampoline and still layin' into 'im with that cane and you could 'ear the bones being snapped, I really could 'ear 'em. And 'is body was like it was jumpin' about on the roadway. And that was all. It was terrible. I can't remember nuffink else. I think I must've fainted.

*Cross leaves the dock and **Newcomen** is shown into it.*

PRESENTER Inspector Newcomen. You took on this murder case.

NEWCOMEN *(with some pride)* I did. And once the body had been identified I soon realised that this was an extremely important case.

PRESENTER *(to the panel)* Inspector Bennett, perhaps you would like to question your Victorian counterpart?

BENNETT I would. Inspector Newcomen, how was the body identified?

NEWCOMEN Once Miss Cross had called the police, I sent two officers to the scene. My men looked through the victim's possessions and amongst them we found an envelope addressed to a Mr Gabriel Utterson. He was the man's lawyer, a very well-known lawyer as it turned out.

BENNETT I see. And did you make a thorough search of the scene?

NEWCOMEN My men were very professional, sir. We found that the old man still had his purse, even his gold watch, so he had not been robbed, we were sure of that.

BENNETT And the murder weapon?

NEWCOMEN We found the cane the girl talked about – or at least half of it – in the gutter. He must've hit the man so hard it just snapped. Anyway we went to see this Mr Utterson first thing in the morning and he was able to identify the body – not a very pleasant task I can tell you.

*Enter **Utterson**. **Newcomen** comes out of the 'dock' for this brief conversation in central acting area. Lights change.*

UTTERSON *(looking shocked)* This man is… was… no less a person than Sir Danvers Carew MP.

NEWCOMEN Carew! Good God, sir! Is it possible? This will make a great deal of noise. But perhaps the suspect was also known to you, this man Hyde?

UTTERSON Do you have a description of him?

NEWCOMEN Small and wicked-looking, is what the maid calls him.

UTTERSON I have no doubt it is the same Mr Hyde. *(looks into his pocket book and takes out his card)* I think you'll find this is his address.

NEWCOMEN I'm much obliged to you, sir.

*Utterson leaves. **Newcomen** goes back to the 'dock'. Studio lights again.*

BENNETT And what did you find at this address?

NEWCOMEN It was in the most dismal quarter of Soho. Not the sort of place a gentleman would want to find himself alone at night – a low sort of area, if you get me.

BENNETT And the house?

NEWCOMEN He'd taken rooms in a cheap lodging house. But according to his landlady, he was hardly ever there. He paid the rent regularly, but he hadn't been at the house for two whole months until the previous day, the day of the murder. She said he'd been in that night, very late, but then gone away in less than an hour.

BENNETT Did she let you search the rooms?

NEWCOMEN That was no problem – I think she was as curious as we were.

BENNETT And what did you find?

NEWCOMEN The place was expensively furnished. Only two rooms, but he lived in real luxury, so he obviously wasn't short of a pound or two. But when we went in, we could tell that the room had been ransacked – clothes all about the floor with the pockets inside out, all the drawers were open and in the grate there was a pile of ashes as if papers had been burned.

BENNETT Could you identify any of the papers?

NEWCOMEN The butt end of a green cheque book for Hyde's account. What's more, behind the door we found the other half of the stick, the rest of the murder weapon.

BENNETT From that point it should have been easy work to catch the man and convict him, if you don't mind my saying.

NEWCOMEN I don't in the slightest. It's just what I thought myself. But the trail just went cold. We sent a man to the bank. We interviewed the neighbours. We searched the city, but not a trace. No family, no employment, he had never been photographed. Nothing. This was one case we never closed.

*Lights fade. In the darkness we can hear the **News Boys** again.*

NEWS BOYS Read all about it!
Special edition!
Shocking murder of MP! Midnight horror!
Read all about it!

65 ▷

Scene Ten

*Lights on Jekyll's laboratory. **Jekyll** sits, his face in his hands. He looks pale and distraught. **Utterson** stands. Offstage, faintly, we can still hear the **News Boys** in the distance.*

UTTERSON You've heard the news, have you? (**Jekyll** *nods.*) And you know the police are looking for Hyde?

JEKYLL The news boys have been crying it in the square.

UTTERSON There is one thing I must know. Carew was my client, but so are you. I need to know what I am doing. Jekyll, have you been mad enough to hide this fellow?

JEKYLL *(upset)* Utterson, I swear to God. I will never set eyes on him again. I am done with him in this world. It is all at an end. And he doesn't need my help. You don't know him as I do. He is safe, quite safe. Mark my words, he will never more be heard of.

UTTERSON You seem pretty sure of him, and for your sake I hope you may be right. If it came to a trial, your name might crop up.

JEKYLL I'm quite sure of him. I have reasons that I cannot share with anyone. But there is one thing on which you may advise me.

UTTERSON Yes?

JEKYLL I have received a letter from Hyde. And… I am at a loss whether I should show it to the police. I'd like you to look at it and judge for me.

UTTERSON Are you worried that it might lead to his detection?

JEKYLL No. I can't say I care what becomes of Hyde; I am quite done with him. But…

UTTERSON Let me see it. *(**Jekyll** hands over the letter. **Utterson** reads it carefully.)* Mmm… Well I would agree with this bit: 'I have repaid you unworthily for the thousand generosities you have shown me' – that's true enough. Do you believe him when he says that he has made his escape and will never be seen in London again?

JEKYLL I do, Utterson.

UTTERSON *(folding the letter)* Do you have the envelope?

JEKYLL I burned it before I knew what it was about. It had no postmark – it must have come by hand.

UTTERSON May I keep this and sleep on it?

JEKYLL I want you to decide. I have lost all confidence in myself.

UTTERSON One more question: about that will of yours – was it Hyde who dictated those terms about your disappearance? (*Jekyll looks frightened. His mouth remains tightly shut. He nods*) I knew it. He meant to murder you for your money. You've had a close escape.

JEKYLL More to the point, I have had a lesson – Oh God, Utterson, what a lesson I have had!

Jekyll covers his face again in despair. *Utterson* looks awkward and leaves the room. As he leaves, *Poole* brings him his coat and hat.

UTTERSON Ah, thank you, Poole. Oh, by the by, that letter handed in today, tell me, what was the messenger like?

POOLE Letter, sir?

UTTERSON Yes, the one for the doctor.

POOLE There has been no letter handed in today, sir.

UTTERSON You're sure?

POOLE Quite sure. There was some post, but only circulars.

UTTERSON Thank you, Poole.

Utterson leaves. *Poole* looks after him, puzzled. Lights fade and come up on the TV studio set.

Scene Eleven

PRESENTER (*to camera*) As luck would have it, Mr Gabriel Utterson was the kind of man who kept his papers in perfect order and destroyed nothing. We've been able to trace this letter from Edward Hyde to Dr Jekyll in Utterson's files and I have a copy of it here. (*The letter is projected on to an OHP screen.*) We have also arranged for a graphologist, an expert in the study of people's handwriting, to be in our studio tonight. We are now calling her as a witness, Pauline Hill. (*Hill is led in by a studio Assistant who guides her to stand by the OHP*) Good evening, Ms Hill.

HILL Good evening.

PRESENTER First, could you confirm that you have heard nothing of the story behind this week's 'Strange Case' ?

HILL No, nothing at all.

PRESENTER So you don't know the identity of the writer of this handwriting sample?

HILL No.

PRESENTER Would you be able to make some observations about the sample?

HILL I would say... a man's writing... quite a young man. It's quite an unusual style, the pen seems to be gripped very hard. Er... the cramped style and the retracing of some letters might suggest that he was rather a repressed personality...

PRESENTER You say repressed? Would you go any further? Could this be the writing of someone who was disturbed, even psychotic?

HILL *(laughing)* No, not from this. An odd style, maybe, but hardly psychotic.

PRESENTER Out of interest, could you compare the handwriting with this second sample?

Assistant places part of a letter from Henry Jekyll on the OHP. It ends with his signature. We can see it beside the Hyde letter.

HILL I would say he wrote this when he was older, this Henry... Jekyll, is it? You can still see a number of identical features, the strange loops on these 'g's, for instance. Interestingly, the slant is different.

PRESENTER But these are written by two different men.

HILL Oh no. There's little doubt that the same man wrote them. In fact, I'd be certain of it.

PRESENTER Thank you, Pauline Hill.

The OHP is turned off and the Assistant leads Hill off.

PRESENTER *(to the panel)* So, what do we make of that?

FALLON It looks as if Jekyll forged the letter to himself. But why?

BENNETT Perhaps he wanted to throw the police off Hyde's trail.

PRESENTER *(to camera)* With or without the letter, the police continued to have no success in tracking down Hyde, despite offering huge rewards for information leading to his arrest. Rumours spread linking Hyde to a string of other violent crimes, but there was no hard information. Mr Utterson's memoirs take up the story for us.

Spotlight on **Utterson** *in the dock.*

UTTERSON For a few months after the death of Carew, Jekyll seemed more relaxed and happy than I had known him for two years. He seemed to have begun a new life now that Hyde's evil influence had left. He came out of his shell, spent more time with friends, even threw some parties. He involved himself more in his charity work. And then a few months later, in January of 1884, something changed. It was as if he had shut his door on the world. Whenever I visited the house it was always the same story.

Scene Twelve

Lights on main stage. **Utterson** *knocks on the door.* **Poole** *opens it.*

POOLE Good morning, Mr Utterson.

UTTERSON Morning, Poole. Will your master see me today?

POOLE I'm sorry, sir. He will see no one.

UTTERSON Again? Tell him it's me who is calling. Surely he will give me a minute of his time.

POOLE He will not leave the laboratory for anyone, sir. He says... he does not dare leave it.

UTTERSON What? Is he still confined to that laboratory of his? Doesn't dare leave it? What can he be doing in there? Working on some experiment? Do you think he's ill?

POOLE I cannot tell, sir. I have not seen him for days now. He has even taken to sleeping in there. He has his meals left outside the door. He has become a total recluse.

UTTERSON But you must speak with him sometimes?

POOLE Hardly ever. He has grown very silent. I fear he is very down, sir.

UTTERSON This is strange, Poole. I think I need to speak to Dr Lanyon about it. If Jekyll is unwell, perhaps Lanyon can help him.

Lights fade on main stage. **Utterson** *walks to studio 'dock'.*

PRESENTER And you went to visit Lanyon?

UTTERSON The same day.

PRESENTER Was he able to help you?

UTTERSON Not at all. In fact, Hastie Lanyon was in an even worse way than my friend Jekyll.

Lights fade on studio. They come up to reveal **Lanyon** *on main acting area. The scene is set in Lanyon's study, as on page 16. He looks pale, older than before. His hair is dishevelled and his eyes look sunken. He stares ahead.* **Utterson** *moves to join him.*

LANYON I have had a shock. *(long pause)* I have had a shock and I shall never recover.

UTTERSON Never recover? Of course you will, Hastie, old man.

LANYON *(ignoring him and staring ahead)* I am not long for this world. It is a question of weeks. Well, I have enjoyed my life. I used to enjoy it. *(pause)* I sometimes think if we knew all, we should be glad to get away.

Long pause.

UTTERSON Jekyll is ill too. Have you seen him?

LANYON *(reacting strongly and holding up a hand)* I wish to see or hear no more of Dr Jekyll. I am quite done with that... person. Don't ever mention him again – I regard him as dead.

UTTERSON Can't I do something? We are three very old friends, Lanyon.

LANYON Nothing can be done. Ask him.

UTTERSON He will not see me.

LANYON That doesn't surprise me. Some day, Utterson, after I am dead, you may perhaps find out the truth, but right now I cannot tell you. But, I ask you, never mention his name again. I cannot bear it.

Lights fade. They come up again on the TV studio. **Utterson** *returns to the dock.*

Scene Thirteen

PRESENTER *(to camera)* Within two weeks of that interview, Lanyon was dead. And with his will, he left a sealed envelope to Utterson marked as 'not to be opened till the death or disappearance of Dr Henry Jekyll'. You will note yet another reference to the 'disappearance' of Jekyll. Later tonight, 'Strange Cases' will be able to reveal, for the first time, the contents of that envelope sent by Dr Lanyon. But first we take up the extraordinary events of that January and follow them to their tragic conclusion.

Music. Fade to blackout as the **Producer** *calls for a break and house lights.*

ACT TWO

Scene One

The TV studio.

PRODUCER OK, everybody. Can we have the floor ready? Lights on the dock. We'll cut straight into Utterson's story of the last night. Can we have Utterson on the set, please?

Utterson enters and goes into the dock.

PRODUCER And, action!

UTTERSON It was only a few days after Dr Lanyon's funeral. One evening after dinner, I was surprised to receive a visit from Poole, Dr Jekyll's servant. The moment I saw him, I knew that there was something wrong.

FALLON How could you tell?

UTTERSON The man was in a state of terror, very agitated. He told me that his master, Jekyll, had been locked up in his laboratory for days and days.

FALLON Perhaps Jekyll was ill – or working on some complicated experiment?

UTTERSON Exactly what I said. But Poole was very frightened and insisted that I went to the house with him straight away. Only when we got there and stood outside the door of Jekyll's office did Poole share his worst fears with me.

Utterson leaves the dock and takes the stage with Poole.

Scene Two

POOLE I've been afraid for about a week and I can bear it no more.

UTTERSON Poole, I can see this is something serious. Try to tell me what it is.

POOLE I think there's been foul play. Follow me. I want you to hear, and I don't want you to be heard. And see here, sir, if by any chance he was to ask you in, don't go.

Poole knocks uncertainly on the laboratory door. We hear a voice reply.

POOLE Mr Utterson, sir, asking to see you.

HYDE *(harshly)* Tell him I cannot see anyone.

POOLE Thank you, sir. *(to **Utterson**)* Was that my master's voice?

UTTERSON It seems much changed.

POOLE Changed? Well, I should think so. Have I been twenty years in this man's house to be deceived about his voice? No, sir; master's been made away with.

UTTERSON You mean... murdered?

POOLE I do, sir. He was made away with eight days ago; and who's in there instead of him, and why it stays there, God only knows, Mr Utterson.

UTTERSON This is a wild tale, Poole. Suppose it were as you think – supposing Dr Jekyll to have been well, murdered – what could induce the murderer to stay? That won't hold water. It makes no sense.

POOLE All this week, he – or it – or whatever it is that lives in that room has been crying out for some sort of medicine. Writing his orders on a piece of paper and throwing it out on the stair here. Nothing but papers, and a closed door and the meals left there to be smuggled in when nobody was looking.

UTTERSON And he's sent you to find this medicine?

POOLE Every day, ay, and twice and thrice in the same day, there have been orders and complaints, and I have been sent flying to all the wholesale chemists in town. Every time I brought the stuff back, there would be another note telling me to return it, because it was not pure enough, and another order to a different firm. This drug is wanted bitter bad, sir, whatever for.

UTTERSON Do you have any of these notes?

Poole pulls a crumpled note from his pocket and hands it to **Utterson**. *He looks at it closely. We hear* **Hyde's** *voice cry out from inside the room.*

Hyde *(offstage)* For God's sake, find me some of the old stuff.

Utterson It certainly looks like Jekyll's handwriting.

Poole What does the handwriting matter? I've seen him!

Utterson Seen him?

Poole I think he must have slipped out to look for his drug. He was in the yard outside the laboratory. When he saw me, he gave a kind of cry and whipped up the steps. It was only for a minute that I saw him but the hair on my head stood up like quills.

Utterson You were afraid?

Poole Sir, if that was my master, why had he a mask upon his face? If it was my master, why did he cry out like a rat and run from me? I have served him long enough.

Utterson Perhaps your master is suffering from some hideous illness which has deformed his features and altered his voice. Hence the mask and his avoidance of his friends; hence his eagerness to find this drug and

Poole Oh, sir, do you think I don't know my master after twenty years? No sir, that thing in the mask was never Dr Jekyll. God knows what it was, but it was never Dr Jekyll; and it is the belief of my heart that there was murder done.

Utterson Poole, if you say that, we must make certain. I shall consider it my duty to break down the door.

Poole Ah, Mr Utterson, that's talking!

Utterson And now comes another question. Who's going to do it?

Poole Why, you and me, sir.

Utterson Good man, Poole.

Poole There is an axe in the yard.

Poole runs off. We hear **Hyde** *cry out from behind the door.*

34

Hyde Lost forever!

Poole returns with an axe and a heavy poker.

Poole Here. Take the kitchen poker for yourself.

Utterson You know, Poole, that you and I are about to put ourselves in some danger? *(Poole nods)* Well, we might as well say what we think. *(pause)* This masked figure that you saw — did you recognise it?

Poole Well, sir, it went so quick, and the creature was so doubled up, that I could hardly swear to it. But if you mean, was it Mr Hyde – why, yes, I think it was! It was the same size and it had the same quick, light way with it. And who else could have got in the laboratory door? After all, at the time of the murder he still had the key with him. But that's not all. Have you ever met this Mr Hyde?

Utterson Yes. Once.

Poole There was something about the man, something… I don't rightly know how to say it, sir, beyond this: that you felt in your marrow – kind of cold and thin.

Utterson I admit I felt that way too.

Poole When that masked thing like a monkey jumped up and ran away from me, it went down my spine like ice. I would swear on the Bible it was Mr Hyde.

Utterson I fear it too. Evil was sure to come of that connection. Ay, truly, I believe you, I believe poor Harry is killed. And I believe his murderer is still lurking in his victim's room. Well, let our name be vengeance!

*We hear **Hyde** pacing up and down. He cries out again.*

Hyde *(cries out offstage)* The horror!

Poole So it will walk all day – and the better part of the night.

Utterson Is there never anything else?

POOLE Once. Once I heard it weeping.

UTTERSON Weeping?

POOLE Weeping like a woman or a lost soul. I came away with that upon my heart, that I could have wept too.

UTTERSON Come. It's time to settle this. *(shouts)* Jekyll! I demand to see you. *(pause)* I must see you! If not by fair means, then by foul.

Pause. **Utterson** *and* **Poole** *look at one another.* **Utterson** *nods and* **Poole** *raises the axe.*

UTTERSON *(shouts)* Let us in or we will use brute force.

HYDE Utterson! For God's sake have mercy!

UTTERSON Ah, that's not Jekyll's voice – it's Hyde's. Down with the door, Poole!

Utterson *and* **Poole** *start to break down the door.* **Hyde** *screams.*

Utterson *and* **Poole** *force their way in. The body of* **Hyde** *lies face down on the floor, twitching. In his hand* **Hyde** *has a glass phial.* **Utterson** *goes over to the body and stands over it. (This moment is repeated at the end of the play as a freeze.)* **Utterson** *turns the body over.*

UTTERSON Hyde! *(takes the phial from Hyde's hand)* Suicide. It only remains for us to find the body of your master. *(***Utterson** *and* **Poole** *search the laboratory)* Jekyll must be here.

Poole *stamps the floor.*

POOLE He must be buried here.

UTTERSON Or he may have fled. Try the door.

Utterson *goes to the door. Stoops down and picks up the key. It is broken.*

UTTERSON Broken! He can't have used this. This is beyond me.

POOLE A man can't disappear into thin air.

UTTERSON *(going over to the laboratory table)* Perhaps his desk will give us some clue.

POOLE This is the same drug that I was always bringing him.

UTTERSON So many ...

POOLE *(looking into the mirror)* This mirror has seen some strange things, sir.

UTTERSON None stranger than itself. What could Jekyll want with it?

POOLE You can say that. Sir! Sir! Some papers.

UTTERSON I'll take those, Poole. Remember, I am his lawyer.

*Poole hands them over. **Utterson** reads them.*

POOLE What do they say, sir?

UTTERSON My head is spinning. This makes no sense. Why didn't Hyde destroy this?

POOLE *(picking up another piece of paper and handing it over)* Sir. Another note.

UTTERSON Oh, Poole! Jekyll was alive and here today. He wrote this recently. He can't have been disposed of in so short a space. He must be alive. He must have fled!

POOLE Alive? But then, what about Hyde? Has he... been...

UTTERSON Perhaps it is not suicide. Oh, we must be careful. I fear there may yet be worse in store for Jekyll.

POOLE Why don't you read the papers, sir?

UTTERSON Because I fear. God grant I have no cause for it. *(puts the paper in his pocket)* Say nothing about these papers. If your master has fled or is dead, we can at least save his reputation.

POOLE Yes, sir.

UTTERSON It is now ten. I must go home and read these documents in quiet. I shall be back before midnight and then we shall send for the police. *(turns to go)* And Poole?

POOLE Sir?

UTTERSON Not a word to anyone about the papers.

Lights fade.

Scene Three

*Lights come up on the studio panel. **Utterson** and **Poole** cross over to the dock.*

PRESENTER The inquest passed a verdict of suicide and no trace was ever found of Dr Henry Jekyll. When the police investigated the death of Hyde, they were unable to find his birth certificate or any other official document relating to him. He had never been photographed and there was no record of his ever having been employed. After a few weeks, the investigation ran into the ground. To this day we are unsure of the real identity of this mysterious figure suspected of the murder of Sir Danvers Carew and connected with the sudden disappearance of Dr Henry Jekyll. Mr Gabriel Utterson, who first discovered Hyde's body, remains our most reliable witness. Perhaps we could allow our own detective, Inspector Bennett, to take up the questioning.

BENNETT Thanks. Now, Mr Utterson. I'd like to start with a matter of detail. You discovered the body at ten o'clock that evening.

UTTERSON I did.

BENNETT Yet you went a full two hours before informing the police?

UTTERSON I needed time to make sense of the paperwork. I could hardly believe what I had found. It did not make sense.

BENNETT Can I suggest, with respect, that it's the police's job to make sense of the evidence – not yours. As a lawyer, you must have known your duty to report the crime immediately?

UTTERSON I own that I did. But my head was spinning. The document Poole found concerned me in a way I did not expect.

BENNETT Go on.

UTTERSON It was another will.

BENNETT Different from the first one?

UTTERSON In many ways the same. The same extraordinary clause that it should serve in case of the death – or sudden disappearance – of Dr Jekyll.

BENNETT So how was it different?

UTTERSON Instead of leaving everything to Hyde – in place of the name of Hyde, it had my name. I was staggered.

BENNETT Why? After all, you were his oldest friend.

UTTERSON That's not the point. You see, the document lay open on the desk. And Hyde had been alone in the room for maybe eight days. He had the will in his possession for all that time, he had no cause to like me, but he had not destroyed the document. He could have escaped at any time through the house, even though the key to the outside door of the laboratory was broken.

BENNETT Ah, yes, that key. You say it was broken?

POOLE Yes, sir, as if a man had stamped on it.

BENNETT Any idea how long it had been broken?

POOLE Some time before. The broken part was stained with rust.

BENNETT I see. Let's now turn to the death of Hyde. In your opinion, he had committed suicide?

UTTERSON I took the phial of poison from his grasp. Poole saw me and testified at the inquest.

BENNETT And finally – do you suppose there was any way, perhaps under extreme provocation, maybe blackmail, maybe something related to his desperation to get hold of this unknown drug, that Jekyll might have murdered Hyde?

UTTERSON Out of the question.

POOLE Dr Jekyll was not a violent man.

PRESENTER Perhaps I could just bring in Rosalyn Croft here on the drugs issue. *(to* **Croft***)* Is it possible that a respectable Victorian gentleman could really be mixed up in some kind of experiment with dangerous drugs?

CROFT Well, the end of the nineteenth century was a time when experimentation with drugs was more widespread than we might like to think nowadays.

PRESENTER Are we talking about the kind of substances we would now call hard drugs?

CROFT Absolutely. Opium derivatives, like morphine and even heroin were used freely for pain relief, to such an extent that they were a mainstay of Victorian medicine. Many other people experimented with their use – like the writer Coleridge or, another example, the fictional character of Sherlock Holmes. Oh yes, it was quite common.

PRESENTER Presumably it was against the law.

CROFT Well, surprisingly it wasn't. There were quite strict laws against drunkenness, but no drugs legislation yet. In fact, the only way people could be prosecuted was if it could be proved that the drug had been taken as a drink. Substances now classified as Class A drugs could be bought in opium dens. Drug-taking was dangerous but not illegal.

PRESENTER Is it possible that the drugs angle gives us an explanation for the strange relationship between Jekyll and this shady character, Hyde? Perhaps he was acting as a supplier, a link to the underworld of the opium dens?

CROFT Quite possibly. After all, a respectable man like Jekyll would not have wanted to visit opium dens if he could help it. These were risky places and the health risks were many. So, certainly, yes, it would be handy to have a runner.

PRESENTER Thank you.

FALLON I should like to ask Mr Poole something. *(Poole nods)* It was you who found the will that we have talked about?

POOLE All the papers were lying on my master's table.

FALLON You mean there was more than one set of papers?

POOLE *(guiltily)* Er… yes… but it was Mr Utterson's decision. I felt he knew what was best.

FALLON Mr Utterson?

UTTERSON It was a personal document, addressed to me.

PRESENTER But surely it related to the case? You concealed this from the inquest?

UTTERSON I was compromised. Remember, I was Jekyll's lawyer too. If we had found Jekyll, if there had been a murder trial, well then I would have brought the papers forward. But I could only see them causing harm to my client's reputation.

PRESENTER Why? Was this a confession to the murder of Hyde?

UTTERSON Absolutely not. It was more of a statement of the events leading up to it. I do not know what could have induced Henry Jekyll to write such crazed ravings. He was unhinged.

PRESENTER So what did you do with this... statement?

UTTERSON I kept it locked away with the other papers given me by Dr Lanyon.

*Lights fade on all characters except for the **Presenter** who talks to camera.*

PRESENTER *(to camera)* And that's how things stayed for over a hundred years – a spine-tingling tale, one of many unclosed cases from Victorian London. Until, earlier this year, a firm of city solicitors came across an interesting file in their archives. The file contained a number of legal documents belonging to a lawyer who had once been a partner in the firm. He died in 1908. This lawyer was none other than our key witness, Mr Gabriel Utterson, whose part has been so ably played for us tonight by [*name of actor*]. On close inspection the papers proved to be the very same missing documents – the statements from Dr Hastie Lanyon and Dr Henry Jekyll.

For the first time tonight, 'Strange Cases' can reveal the contents of those statements. The story they tell is not for the faint of heart and our reconstruction is based faithfully on the words of both Lanyon and Jekyll. As we have suggested, Jekyll was disturbed, possibly even unhinged, at the time of his disappearance. We cannot verify what he – or Lanyon – has written. We can simply present the new evidence and leave you, the audience, to judge for yourselves.

Scene Four

*Haunting music. Lights fade to blackout and then come up to reveal Jekyll's laboratory. The **Chorus** stands in two groups, one on each side of the stage. **Jekyll** is in the laboratory. There is a table with flasks, condensers and other scientific apparatus (e.g. a large machine for some kind of electrical experiment). A magic lantern is set up on the table. There is a large mirror in a frame. **Jekyll** is writing at the table.*

JEKYLL Here follows the full statement of Dr Henry Jekyll. Do not judge me until you have heard my tale for if I am the chief of sinners, I am the chief of sufferers also. Here in this laboratory my experiments into transcendental medicine have taken me into a new province of knowledge…

*Some of the lines spoken by the **Chorus** are divided between the two groups, numbered **C1** and **C2**.*

CHORUS and into the darkest blackness of distress.

C1 Dr Jekyll, who tasted from the cup of pure pleasure …

C2 and was thrown into an abyss of terror and despair.

JEKYLL *(rising from the desk)* I could not think this earth contained a place for sufferings and terrors so unmanning. And here, in my own laboratory, where I once pushed back the frontiers of science, I must now end my days as a miserable prisoner. *(cries)* Oh, God, is there no way out for me? Time is running out. I must tell my story.

*Jekyll turns on the magic lantern. He projects an image of himself on to a backdrop. During the next sequence the **Chorus** enacts the images of the two sides of Jekyll.*

CHORUS Henry Jekyll, M.D., D.C.L., Fellow of the Royal Society

C1 A pillar of society,
Renowned for his charitable works, and his religion.

C2 But then there was a darker side to Dr Jekyll,
The doctor who haunted the backstreets of Soho,
And trawled the taverns and opium dens.

C1 An upright man, known for his restraint

C2 But who plunged himself in shame.

Chorus A double-dealer.

Jekyll A double-dealer, yes! I admit it. But not a hypocrite. I admit it all, but both sides of me were truly me – the good and the bad. I couldn't help either. But then my scientific studies led me steadily towards the discovery that man is not truly one...

Chorus Not truly one,
But truly two.
Two.

C1 Good.

C2 Evil.

C1 Jekyll.

C2 Hyde.

Jekyll holds his hand in front of the magic lantern. We see the bright light shine through his flesh.

Jekyll One night, as I was reflecting on this, I started to wonder if certain chemicals could be made to release our dual identities from the solid prison of our body. And yes, I found that there are certain agents which have the power to separate the two elements within us. Think of the effects of such an experiment.

C2 Our lower nature could go its own way, do what it wants, free from guilt.

C1 And our better half could carry on its upward path, doing good things, with no danger of disgrace.

Jekyll Mankind would be freed from the continuous struggle within...

C1 between good

C2 and evil.

JEKYLL I won't trouble you with the full scientific details of my discoveries, mainly because they have taught me such a bitter lesson, but in the end I managed to compound a drug which I believed would bring my experiment to its conclusion. I knew that I risked death, but I had to put my theories to the test. I bought the final ingredient from a firm of wholesale chemists, a large quantity of a particular salt.

Jekyll pours powder into a chemical container and stirs. The chemicals react.

CHORUS Then, late one accursed night
You mixed the elements,
Watching them boil and smoke together in the glass,
And with a strong glow of courage
You drank off the potion.

JEKYLL I felt the most racking pains.

*Loud music. Flashing lights. **Jekyll** goes to the magic lantern and superimposes an image of **Hyde** over that of **Jekyll**, and then only the image of **Hyde** is projected. In the darkness, **Jekyll** 'disappears'. Then the lights come up slowly to reveal **Hyde** standing in front of the mirror admiring his image. He moves quickly about the stage. The **Chorus** moves with him, speaking over the music.*

56

78–79

C1 A grinding in the bones,
Deadly nausea,
A horror of the spirit.

64

C2 But then the pain subsided and you felt a new sensation …
Something indescribably new,
Incredibly sweet,
You felt younger, lighter, happier in body.

C1 You knew yourself, at the first breath of this new life, to be more wicked, tenfold more wicked, sold a slave to your original evil.

CHORUS And the thought delighted you like wine!

HYDE *(shouting as the music reaches crescendo)* All human beings are a mixture of good and evil: and Edward Hyde, alone, in the ranks of mankind is pure evil!

Silence. Pause. **Hyde** *looks worried.*

HYDE But what if there is no return? If I was trapped forever in this new identity? I would have to escape from this house which would no longer be mine. I must see what happens and try the drug again.

Hyde *drinks the drug. We see a second transformation into the character of* **Jekyll***. This time,* **Jekyll** *admires himself in the mirror and then turns to face first the* **Chorus** *and then the audience.*

56 ▶

78–79 ▶

JEKYLL And so you see, I was master of my own destiny. I made the most careful arrangements. I told my servants that a Mr Hyde was in possession of the key to the laboratory door and was to have the run of my house. I drew up the will that so upset poor Utterson. And then I only had to drink the cup to escape into the world of Edward Hyde. I took the house in Soho to which the police eventually tracked Hyde. But for me, the safety was complete. Think of it – I did not even exist! Give me a second or two to swallow the draught that I always had standing ready and, whatever he had done, Edward Hyde would pass away...

CHORUS Like a stain of breath upon a mirror.

C1 And there instead, quietly at home,
Trimming the midnight lamp in his study,
A man above all suspicion,
Would be Dr Henry Jekyll.

C2 There were nights of selfish pleasure,
Monstrous depravity,
Wild cruelty.

CHORUS You gloried and trembled in your excesses,
Your lust of evil gratified and stimulated.

JEKYLL My love of life forced to the extreme.

CHORUS *(whispered echo)* Life!

The figure of **Hyde** *appears. Dance/movement based on Hyde's adventures, culminating in slow-motion replay of the trampling of the young girl. The* **Doctor**, **Enfield** *etc. are played either by the original actors or by the new* **Chorus***. Throughout the word 'Life' is whispered, chanted, always louder.*

60 ▶

Chorus LIFE!!
You thought you were beyond the reach of fate.
You should have known better, Jekyll.

Jekyll I returned late one night. I had been out for one of my adventures. And when I woke the next morning, I felt different.

Chorus The hand, Jekyll.

Jekyll I thought at first I was in the little room in Soho, Hyde's room...

Chorus The hand...

Jekyll But I recognised my own room, the curtains, the bed frame.

Chorus The hand...

Jekyll And then in my comfortable morning doze, my eye fell upon my hand. It was the hand of Edward Hyde!

C1 You had gone to bed Henry Jekyll...

C2 and awakened Edward Hyde.

Jekyll The power of the drug was beginning to fail me. I doubled the amount. When I began my experiments, the trouble had been to throw off the body of Jekyll; now it was the opposite. I could see the writing on the wall: it was time to stop playing with this transforming drug and make a choice between my two identities.

Chorus Which is it to be?

C1 Jekyll?

C2 Or Hyde?

C1 Cast in your lot with Jekyll...

C2 and say goodbye to all those pleasures and appetites you have so secretly enjoyed. Cast in your lot with Hyde...

C1 and say goodbye to all your interests, and ambitions as a doctor and a scientist. Think how much you have to lose.

C2 Be Hyde. That way you won't even know what you've lost. Choose youth, the light step, leaping pulses, and secret pleasure.

C1 Be Jekyll. Choose your friends, your surgery.

JEKYLL *(shouting)* Jekyll! I will be Jekyll! I will be Jekyll. And so it was for two months until I was tortured –

CHORUS Tempted?

JEKYLL No, I tell you, it wasn't like that. I was tortured with throes and longings, as if Hyde was within me, struggling for freedom.

CHORUS And you prepared the drug again?

JEKYLL Yes, yes I took it! I was unable to reason. The spirit of hell awoke in me and raged. My devil had been caged –

Hyde runs in.

HYDE *(shouting)* – And it came out roaring!

CHORUS Roaring for blood.

HYDE Violence!

CHORUS Destruction!

HYDE Murder!

CHORUS And Sir Danvers Carew.

Scene Five

*Enter **Carew**. He is elderly, smartly dressed. He stops and greets **Hyde**, raising his hat.*

CAREW Good evening, sir.

HYDE *(squaring up to him)* You think so, do you? You think it's a good evening do you?

CAREW Would you be so kind as to give me the time?

HYDE I'll give you nothing of the sort.

*Music and strobe as **Hyde** launches a brutal assault on **Carew**. He hits him repeatedly with his stick and kicks the body across the stage. When he has finished, he punches the air in triumph.*

HYDE Life!

***Hyde** holds the pose like a statue. **Jekyll** breaks down beside him and kneels.*

CHORUS Special edition.
    Read all about it!
    Midnight horror!
    Shocking murder of MP!

JEKYLL *(shouting)* No-o-o-!! Death! Murder! Blood on my hands!
    Oh God, forgive me.

CHORUS Too late now, Jekyll.
    Everything is gone now. Think back to your childhood, when you walked holding your father's hand.

JEKYLL No, no, no.

C1 All your good works as a doctor.

C2 All blotted out by the damned horrors of that night.

JEKYLL No. It was Hyde. It was not me. And now Hyde can no longer exist. *(**Jekyll** smiles and takes out the key to the laboratory)* At least I now have no choice. After this, Hyde will be hunted in every corner of the land,

CHORUS A known murderer,
    Thrall to the gallows.
    Why, if he was to step outside for a minute, he would be instantly arrested!

JEKYLL I shall lock the laboratory door by which he comes and goes and so lock Hyde away forever!

***Jekyll** goes to lock the door, returns and drops the key to the floor. He grinds it under his heel until it is broken.*

48

CHORUS If only it was so easy, Jekyll.
Hyde had been indulged for so long that he could not be
locked away.
And now your darker side was growling for release.
The animal within you licking the chops of memory.
It happened again.

JEKYLL Outside the house. One fine, clear January day, in Regent's
Park. I was sitting in the sun on a bench. A qualm came over me,
a horrid nausea and the most deadly shuddering. I could sense
the change sweeping over me – a surge of courage, a contempt
for everyone around me. I was once more Edward Hyde. I also
sensed the danger.

CHORUS The drugs were in the laboratory,
But the door was closed
And the key destroyed.
You needed someone else.
So you thought of Lanyon
And dragged him down into the pit with you.

JEKYLL I, or rather Hyde, sent Lanyon a letter from Dr Jekyll. It
gave him authority to break down the laboratory door and
instructions to take the drawer with all the drugs back to his
house. The letter gave away no secrets – he didn't need to know
the truth! It only set out my plan to bring the drugs.

Scene Six

Jekyll exits. Enter **Lanyon**. *He is reading from the letter.*

LANYON 'At midnight, I ask you to be alone in your consulting
room and to admit with your own hand into your house a man
who will present himself in my name. Place in his hands the
drawer that you will have brought from my laboratory. Lanyon,
my life, my honour, my reason, depend upon you. If you will
just help me, my troubles will roll away like a story that is told.
Serve me, my dear Lanyon, and save

Your friend,

H. J. '

*As he reaches the end of the letter, the clock strikes twelve and there is a violent knocking at the door. **Lanyon** goes and re-enters with **Hyde** who looks desperate, searching about the room for the drawer.*

LANYON Are you come from Dr Jekyll?

HYDE Have you got it? Have you got it?

LANYON Come sir, you forget that we have not met before. Be seated.

*Lanyon sits. **Hyde** sits. Then jumps up.*

HYDE *(urgently)* I come here from Dr Jekyll. On a piece of urgent business. I understood... *(he searches again)* I understood, a drawer.

LANYON *(pointing)* There it is, sir.

***Hyde** springs on the drawer greedily.*

LANYON Compose yourself.

***Hyde** snarls at him.*

HYDE Fetch me a glass. A graduated glass.

*Lanyon fetches a glass while **Hyde** starts to prepare the drug. **Lanyon** returns and **Hyde** pours chemicals into the glass, adding the powder last of all. He mutters to himself all the while. He ignores **Lanyon's** questions.*

LANYON Do you know what you are doing, sir? I'm a medical man, you know. Is that phosphorus I smell? And that's ether, if I'm not mistaken.

HYDE *(muttering)* And now to add this... so... it must be double... double measures... there!

*The chemicals change colour in the glass and **Hyde** looks triumphant.*

HYDE And now to settle what remains. You can leave the room now and you will be left as you were before, neither wiser nor richer. Or has the greed of curiosity got the better of you, eh? You could leave me. Or, if you so choose, stay and watch. New avenues to fame and power shall be laid open to you, here, in this room; and your sight shall be blasted by a prodigy to stagger the unbelief of Satan. Well?

LANYON Sir, your riddles don't impress me. But I have gone along with this so far, I shall see the end.

HYDE Oh yes? You, who for so long denied the value of my research, you who derided your superiors – behold!

*Transformation to **Jekyll**.*

56

LANYON *(screaming)* Oh God! Oh God! Jekyll!

78–79

CHORUS A week afterwards Dr Lanyon took to his bed.
And in something less than a fortnight he was dead.
He had looked into the face of horror and his days were counted.

JEKYLL I reached the shelter of my laboratory, close to my drugs, but within six hours the effect had worn off. Again it took a double dose to recall me to myself. And so it went on. Every few hours the pangs returned and the drug had to be re-administered until it was only under the immediate effect of the chemicals that I was able to wear the identity of Jekyll. At all hours of day and night it would happen; above all, if I slept, or even dozed for a moment in my chair, it was always as Hyde that I awakened. I am a prisoner.

Scene Seven

*A knocking at the door. We hear **Poole's** (and later **Utterson's**) voice from the other side of the door.*

JEKYLL Who's there?

POOLE *(offstage)* Mr Utterson, sir, asking to see you.

JEKYLL *(harshly)* Tell him I cannot see anyone.

POOLE Yes, sir.

CHORUS And then the final calamity came
To sever you from your own face and nature.

Jekyll My provision of the salt began to run low. I sent out for a fresh supply and mixed the draught. The mixture bubbled, the colour changed; I drank it. It didn't work. I sent Poole to ransack the town for more, but in vain. I now believe that my first supply was impure and that it was the unknown impurity which aided my discovery. *(shouts)* For God's sake, find me some of the old! *(pause)* Time fails me now. I have taken my last dose. This is the last time that Henry Jekyll can think his own thoughts or see his own face in the mirror. *(looks in mirror)*

Chorus Time fails you.

Jekyll I must not sleep or Jekyll will be lost forever. Lost to the horror of my other self. And this, I tell you, is the shocking thing: that the slime of the pit seems to utter cries and voices.

Chorus Voices, voices…

Jekyll *(cries out in anguish)* The horror!

C1 Knit to you closer than a wife,

C2 Closer than an eye.

C1 Jekyll sobs and cries out,

C2 Caged in your flesh,

C1 Where it mutters and struggles to be born.

C2 And at every hour of weakness

C1 In the confidences of slumber

C2 It will rise up against you

C1 And depose you from your life,
Your sickly, miserable life.

C2 Not like Hyde – he knows how to live!

Jekyll But he fears my power to cut him off by suicide! If needs be, I shall do that. *(holds up a phial)* I have the poison to kill us both. And yet I find it in my heart to pity him; his love of life is so wonderful!

Utterson Jekyll! I demand to see you.

C1 Time fails you.

UTTERSON I must see you! If not by fair means, then by foul.

JEKYLL This is the hour of my death. I feel the throes of change. I will soon be Hyde.

*Jekyll starts to growl and move like **Hyde**.*

C2 Will Hyde die upon the scaffold?

C1 Or will he find the courage to release himself at the last moment?

UTTERSON Let us in, or we will use brute force!

JEKYLL Utterson! For God's sake, have mercy!

UTTERSON Ah, that's not Jekyll's voice – it's Hyde's! Down with the door, Poole!

*Noise of door being smashed down. Four blows of the axe. The lights flash as **Jekyll** takes the phial of poison and screams.*

JEKYLL This is the end!

*Jekyll collapses to floor, face down. **Utterson** and **Poole** burst in. **Poole** is holding the axe. **Utterson** goes over to the body and bends over to turn the body. They freeze in the exact position as on page 36. Fade to blackout.*

THE END

Staging the Play

The theatrical elements of space or lack of space, light and dark, sound and silence, all need to be considered to reinforce the effect of the play upon the audience. Thoughtful use of costume, properties and the overall set will also enhance dramatic impact.

SPACE

The space needs to be used very much like a real TV studio setting which involves a real audience. If the performance space includes a stage area, this would be best used to raise the audience whilst the performers act on the floor below. With the addition of layers on and in front of the stage, the overall effect should be quite authentic.

If the performance space is flat, the audience would need to be on one side, preferably raked, with the action taking place opposite. As the space should imply a real studio, there can be specific areas for the presenter, the panel, the witnesses, the Victorian re-enactments and the laboratory. All the performers can be on set all of the time, along with lighting engineers, sound engineers, stagehands etc. As in a real studio, lighting will direct the attention of the audience from one part of the set to another.

The last part of the play (Act Two, Scene Four onwards) is set only in Jekyll's laboratory. It is therefore possible to use the whole stage for the laboratory, use the chorus as the outside walls and allow for more space for dancers and special effects.

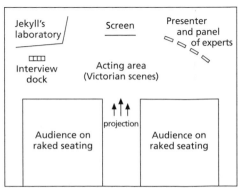

A possible stage set for Act One

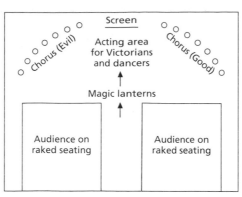

A possible set ground plan for Jekyll's laboratory. (Act Two, Scene Four)

LIGHTING AND SPECIAL EFFECTS

The lighting could be as simple as a single spot to follow the action, thus helping the audience direct their attention. However, the more lighting available the more visually effective the end results will be. Bright lighting could be directed onto the panel and presenter; low lighting could be used for the London scenes with other areas blacked out; and low, coloured lighting could give an eerie glow to the laboratory scenes.

The use of smoke or dry ice would enhance the foggy street scenes. A strobe effect could be used to make the Jekyll to Hyde transformations or the violent scenes more dramatic.

With a video camera and TV or screen projections, the set could be made to look more realistic as a TV studio with monitor screens. For example, the laboratory scenes could be made more interesting by focusing in close-up on important symbols in the story – the potion, the hand, the key, the mirror, the door. With the added technology of a video producer machine, these images could be collaged, distorted, changed in colour or staggered on the screen. If using a large screen, link up video camera to video projector and project images and close-ups of the actors as they are being interviewed. This will add authenticity to the TV studio environment.

The idea of a magic lantern is used in the script as a visual, theatrical and typically Victorian way of changing Jekyll into Hyde by using transparencies that are projected onto a screen. The appearance of magic lanterns in the late 1890s marked the beginning of people's fascination for projected images, which was to lead to the huge movie industry of today.

WARNING: Do not use a strobe light for long periods as it can affect people with certain medical conditions. On posters and programmes add a warning that a strobe light will be used during the performance.

Activities

A. In pairs Choose any scene and outline ideas for the lighting and special effects you would use if given access to all possible technology.

B. In groups The transformation from Jekyll to Hyde is a problem to solve for any live performance. Brainstorm different methods.

- How could you use lighting and special effects to help an actor or actors make the change from Jekyll into Hyde?
- Which is the most effective and suitable method, given the restrictions of your space, finances or available technology?
- Which is the most effective method, given all the resources you would like to have in the professional world of theatre? (See pages 78–79 for more transformation activities.)

C. As a class View a film version or different film versions of the 'Jekyll and Hyde' story on video. Observe how lighting and special effects are used. If possible compare and contrast an old film with a more modern version.

D. In groups If your production requires a magic lantern, how will this be acquired/made? Can you design a way of using modern technology for the lantern but disguise it inside a Victorian frame?

PROPERTIES

If you are staging a simple production, all you will need are chairs for a panel, a standing area for interviewing and a table with symbolic experimental equipment (test tubes, chemical bottles and jars, siphons etc.) plus a mirror for the laboratory.

To go to the other extreme, no end of technological equipment could be used in the TV studio, together with scientific equipment in the laboratory. Boom microphones, TV monitors, projection screens, people moving cameras, audience cue cards would convey the idea that the whole programme was being recorded and televised.

In the scenes within rooms, you could suggest a Victorian room, using a few props, such as an armchair, a table with old gas lamp, old books, clock and rug.

Activities

A. In pairs Make a list of the props needed for part of/the whole of the play.

B. On your own Design or draw part or all of the set, showing the position of the props you have chosen.

C. In groups The potion experiment is another problem to be overcome when staging the play. Investigate the possibilities of which chemicals could be used effectively and safely on stage. Do not experiment without adult supervision!

H

COSTUMES

Costumes need to be in keeping with the overall design of the production. If a basic, simple, minimalist effect is desired, black, white or grey garments could be used with the addition of 'symbolic' accessories such as a police badge or truncheon, a waistcoat, a shawl, a white collar and cravat.

On the other hand, the present-day characters could be dressed in today's fashion and the Victorian characters in typical Victorian costume. Whichever method is chosen, it is usually a good idea to use a narrow and careful blend of colours. Begging old clothes and material from parents, buying from charity shops and then dyeing materials by machine in bulk, can often be a cheap and successful way of adapting clothes into what is required. If the paint or curtains in the performance space are going to form the backdrop, make sure that chosen colours are matched well with these.

Design

Choose a character from the play and design a costume for them which is in keeping with their character. Consider the period, colours and the style. Is it possible to make this costume by recycling clothes or materials?

cont p.59...

Photos from a variety of films, dating from 1920 to 1996, showing different approaches to costume

A. On your own Look through a TV magazine. How many period pieces of theatre or films are on during a week? Watch any period-costume programmes and note the use of design, materials, make-up, colour, setting and lighting.

H

B. As a class Look at the collage of pictures from films of *Dr Jekyll and Mr Hyde* on page 58. Design a poster for a film or theatre production of *Jekyll and Hyde*, using details from the pictures to help you. Think carefully about how the words on the poster will appear. Look at magazines to find examples of different kinds of lettering that you might use.

SOUND

The use of music and sound effects can add depth, atmosphere and interest for the audience. Try to find music on CD or cassette that is suitable for each scene. Many movie soundtracks are now available, giving a wide choice of modern and period instrumental music. Look out for horror or sci-fi movie soundtracks in particular. (See the resource list on page 95–96 for some suggestions.) Most large music shops allow you to listen to any CD in stock, so that you can see if they are suitable. Live or recorded sound effects could be added to any music chosen.

Activities

A. In groups Think about the kinds of music you could use within the play:

- A theme tune for the TV series 'Strange Cases';
- Sound effects for the laboratory scene;
- Transformation music;
- Music for the Victorian street scene;
- Music to divide different sections of the play.

cont...

Devise simple pieces of music for the play. Try using the same chord sequence for each composition but treating the different pieces in different ways – changing the rhythm, the speed, the use of instruments etc. This will also make it easier for you and your musicians to play.

B. On your own How does the use of music and sound effects influence the action of a film and your response to it? Try turning down the volume on your TV and watch the action. What does the music add to the film? If you have access to a video, choose different kinds of music and play them alongside the silent film to see what effect the music has upon you as an audience. Write a report on your findings.

CHOREOGRAPHY

Movement can be used in lots of ways in the play, to create street scenes, or the bustle of the TV studio. The street scenes need to be lively and could include a lot of bystanders, who would need to be well positioned so as to enhance, rather than detract from the focus of attention. The positions on stage of the chorus, and the way they move when talking, will add to the atmosphere of Jekyll's laboratory scene.

Dance is specifically mentioned in the play during the laboratory scene as a means of portraying Hyde's evil adventures. The dance can be choreographed in any style you wish to use.

⚙️ Workshop Activities

A. In groups Brainstorm evil deeds that Hyde may well have performed apart from those mentioned in the play. Think of words to describe his evil deeds; separate the words into two lists, one of nouns and one of verbs. Action words (verbs) are a good inspiration for movement. In your groups, make up movements that express the moods of some of the words on your list. Practise the movements until you have all learnt them. Now join the movements together in interesting ways to make a dance sequence, which you can perform in front of the other groups.

cont...

B. In groups Look at the following extract from Stevenson's novel, Jekyll is talking about Hyde:

'My devil had long been caged and came out roaring ... I struck in no more reasonable spirit than that in which a sick child may break a plaything ... Instantly the spirit of hell awoke in me and raged. With a transport of glee, I mauled the unresisting body, tasting delight from every blow ... I fled from the scene of these excesses, at once glorying and trembling, my lust of evil gratified and stimulated, my love of life screwed to the topmost peg ... Hastening and harkening in my wake for the steps of the avenger ... He walked fast, hunted by his fears, chattering to himself, skulking through the less frequented thoroughfares ... Once a woman spoke to him, offering, I think a box of lights. He smote her in the face, and she fled.'

Pick out verbs, such as 'caged', 'roaring' and 'break', which suggest movements. Make a movement sequence, as in **A** above, using different directions, levels and speeds to vary the ideas and give quality to the movements. Present this to another group, and see if they can guess which words you are describing.

C. In groups Dance could also be used at the beginning of the play, as on a TV programme introduction. Take images from the play and bring them to life, possibly using silhouettes behind a screen.

- In groups of three, think about using the idea of one dancer being Jekyll and two dancers being his good and bad conscience.

- In pairs, experiment with transforming body shapes from good to evil.

It is a good idea to watch professional dance companies on video to pick up ideas. (See resource ideas on page 96 of this book.)

Activities based on and around the play

TV SETTING

This playscript differs in some ways from the original novel. The playwright wanted to keep as much of the original feel of the text and characters as possible, so many of the words are lifted directly from Stevenson's original. Many readers today already know the outline of the story. Because of this, the playwright did not want to write it in a similar way to the book, nor did he want to use the idea of a narrator telling the audience what happened. He used the idea of a TV studio so that the investigative side of the story would be more noticeable. The modern media setting also gives the audience a fresh view of the story. The audience becomes part of the play in the same way that a real TV chat show or game show involves its studio audience.

Media activities

A. In groups Create a 30-second trailer advertising the play as if it were a real TV show. The trailer can use a variety of drama strategies including narration, still images, titles, clips from the exciting scenes and so on. Your aim is to obtain a huge viewing audience when the programme is shown.

B. In pairs Imagine that the story of *Jekyll and Hyde* is a factual one. Create a 30-second news item for *News at Ten* that explains the details to the public. Assume they know nothing. You must get across the essential facts.

C. As a class The story of *Jekyll and Hyde* has been adapted many times for use in films. (See the resource list on page 91 for some of the titles.) What are the advantages of using film rather than the stage? What are the advantages of using the stage rather than film? Brainstorm the ideas and make a list FOR and AGAINST — theatre versus cinema.

cont...

D. On your own Look at some reviews of TV programmes in newspapers. Make a list of all the adjectives that are used in the reviews. Build on this list to write a review of the *Jekyll and Hyde* episode of 'Strange Cases'.

H

MISSING SCENE – THE VISIT TO THE APOTHECARY

In Stevenson's novel, various pieces of information are given to the reader regarding the potion but the visit to the apothecary is not included. In the novel Dr Lanyon tells Utterson that Hyde

32

'measured out a few minims of the red tincture and added one of the powders. The mixture, which was at first of a reddish hue, began, in proportion as the crystals melted, to brighten in colour, to effervesce audibly, and to throw off small fumes of vapour. Suddenly, and at the same moment, the ebullition ceased, and the compound changed to a dark purple, which faded again more slowly to a watery green.'

The reader also knows that Jekyll kept a written 'record of a series of experiments' and that Poole, his butler, would fetch the necessary chemicals for him. It was purchased from a firm of wholesale chemists. Stevenson describes the chemicals as 'salts'.

 **Drama**

In groups Create the scene in which Poole visits the chemist. Bear in mind:

- How much does Poole know about the potion ingredients?
- Does the chemist have any idea of how the chemical may be used?

Recreate the same scene but now with Poole trying to obtain that particular chemical after having been unsuccessful at previous chemists. How does this change his approach to the chemist? He might need to use persuasive language, or even bribery.

> ✍ **Writing**
>
> **On your own** Imagine yourself to be Poole and keep a diary of your day. Record your thoughts about Jekyll's requests for salts and your visits to the apothecary. Mention your fears about what might have happened to your master, and your feelings abour Mr Hyde. Use Act 2, Scene 2, in the playscript.

THE CHORUS

As in Ancient Greek tragedy, the chorus are present at the end of the play as the Good and Bad sides of Jekyll's conscience. They could be used in a variety of ways physically and visually, as well as orally. They could, for example, form the walls of Jekyll's laboratory (see suggested set plan, page 55) and/or be choreographed to move alongside main characters on stage.

> 🎭 **Drama**
>
> **A. In groups** Use the following piece of the script, spoken by the Chorus, to create suitable movements to reinforce the meaning and visual effect for the audience. Select suitable music to play in the background. (See page 59.)
>
> A grinding in the bones.
> Deadly nausea.
> A horror of the spirit.
> But then the pain subsided and you felt a new sensation
> Something incredibly new,
> Incredibly sweet,
> You felt younger, lighter, happier in body.
> You knew yourself, at the first breath of this new life, to be more wicked, tenfold more wicked, sold a slave to your original evil.
> And the thought delighted you like wine.
>
> **B.** Use the same text and consider how the words can be made more interesting by layering voices, using different volumes, sides of the room, repetition, overlap, pauses etc.
>
> **C.** Combine the movement, music and the orchestrated words together and perform it to your class.

NEWSPAPERS

In the play, the news boys break the dramatic news of Sir Danvers Carew's death. This is before radio and television, of course, so the newspapers would be the first with the story.

✒ **Writing**

Use one of the lines that the newsboys shout out as the headline to an **H** article from a newspaper. Write the article, using details from the play, such as quotations from witnesses or people who knew the victims well; add your own imaginative touches, such as a description of the street where the murder took place.

✒ **Writing**

There are several letters mentioned in the novel and the script. The reader does not know the full content of them. Write your own version of the letter on page 26 of this script. Jekyll has written it as being from Hyde to Jekyll and showed it to Utterson. It should be apologetic in nature, from friend to friend, talk of leaving London forever and maybe mentioning murder or evil deeds. This is the letter which the graphologist, Hill, studies. When you have written the letter, copy it out in the style of handwriting you think Hyde might have used. Hill describes it as 'unusual… pen gripped hard… cramped style… retracing some letters… of repressed personality.'

Life and times of Robert Louis Stevenson

Stevenson was born in Edinburgh in 1850. He was a sickly child and poor health made regular schooling difficult. He was expected to follow the family profession of lighthouse engineering, but agreed to study law at Edinburgh University as a compromise. From his teens, he wanted to write. He decided to learn the writer's craft by imitating the work of others. He rebelled violently against his parents' religion in his early days but became more religious when he was older. His fascination for city low-life in Edinburgh, and the bizarre characters he found there, proved to be rich material for his later stories. Severe breathing problems led to a life of travelling in warmer climates. He met Fanny Osbourne, his future wife, in 1876, in France. She was a married woman, ten years his senior, with two children, and proved to be a lively companion who cared for him through many bouts of serious illness.

The Strange Case of Dr Jekyll and Mr Hyde was written at Bournemouth in 1886 during a period of illness and rest. In 1888, Stevenson set out with his family for the South Seas. The literary world was shocked that he should move abroad at the height of his career. Whilst there he wrote a great deal of fiction, which was greatly influenced by his new environment. He was buried in Samoa where people called him Tusitala, 'The Teller of Tales'.

Stevenson wrote more than 30 books including novels, travel diaries, poetry, plays and collections of stories and essays, some of which were written with other people. Famous works include:

> *Treasure Island*, 1883
> *A Child's Garden of Verses*, 1885
> *Kidnapped*, 1886
> *Underwoods* (poetry), 1887
> *The Black Arrow*, 1888
> *Catriona* (sequel to *Kidnapped*), 1893

Writing & Discussion 🎵 😊

A. In groups People often travel to visit the graves of famous people such as rock stars, authors, royalty. Discuss with others how many different shrines you know that people visit today. The custom of visiting the grave of a famous person goes back many years, for example, Chaucer's *Canterbury Tales* relates the story of a pilgrimage to the shrine of St Thomas à Beckett, who was murdered in Canterbury Cathedral in 1170. If you were to travel to Samoa to visit the resting place of Robert Louis Stevenson, what do you think you might see? What might be the epitaph (a short statement written in someone's memory) on his gravestone? Draw the tombstone and write the epitaph as you think it should be.

B. As a sickly child, Stevenson spent a great deal of time in bed. In his collection of poetry for children, *A Child's Garden of Verse*, there are several dream-like poems where he escapes reality by imagining his bed to be a boat or ship. In 'The Land of Counterpane', his bedcover becomes hills, seas, cities:

> *And sometimes for an hour or so*
> *I watched my leaden soldiers go,*
> *With different uniforms and drills,*
> *Among the bedclothes, through the hills;*
> *And sometimes sent my ships in fleets*
> *All up and down among the sheets;*
> *Or brought my trees and houses out,*
> *And planted cities all about.*
> *I was the giant great and still*
> *That sits upon the pillow-hill,*
> *And sees before him, dale and plain,*
> *The pleasant land of counterpane.*

In his poem, 'The Land of Nod', Stevenson describes the fantasy world he can escape to in sleep:

> *The strangest things are there for me,*
> *Both things to eat and things to see,*
> *And many frightening sights abroad*
> *Till morning in the Land of Nod,*
> *Try as I like to find the way,*
> *I never can get back by day,*
> *Nor can remember plain and clear*
> *The curious music that I hear.*

cont…

WHY DID STEVENSON WRITE *THE STRANGE CASE OF DR JEKYLL AND MR HYDE*?

Robert Louis Stevenson

Stevenson said that the idea for *Jekyll and Hyde* came to him in a dream or nightmare. In a magazine article of 1888, called 'A Chapter on Dreams', he writes that he dreamed of two scenes – 'the scene at the window, and a scene afterwards … in which Hyde, pursued for some crime, took the powder and underwent the change in the presence of his pursuers'. As he was crying out in his sleep at this 'fine bogey tale', his wife woke him up, much to his annoyance. However, he is then supposed to have written the novel in three days, argued about it with his wife, burnt it, started from scratch and finished it again in another three days. Within six weeks the book was ready to go to press. When published in 1886 as a cheap 'shilling shocker', it was a huge success.

Stevenson also stated in the magazine article that he had 'long been trying to write a story on this subject, to find a body, a vehicle, for that strong sense of man's double being which must at times come in upon and overwhelm the mind of every thinking creature.'

This idea of a good and bad side to somebody is a theme of other books he wrote as well as *Jekyll and Hyde*. He had been fascinated as a child by the story of a cabinet maker called Deacon Brodie. He was a respectable cabinet maker during the day but a robber by night. Stevenson wrote the play *Deacon Brodie* with W. E. Henley in 1880 about this robber, who was later hanged.

In *Dr Jekyll and Mr Hyde*, Jekyll says that, 'he had more than a father's interest; Hyde had more than a son's indifference.' Perhaps Stevenson was writing partly about his experiences as the son who rebelled against his father's respectable, successful background.

The names of Jekyll and Hyde may well have been chosen because of the well-known game, 'Hide and Seek'. In the novel, Utterson decides to find out more about Mr Hyde and says, 'If he be Mr Hyde, I shall be Mr Seek.' Jekyll should be pronounced as 'Jee-kill' (a Scottish surname) which supports this notion. However, some people also think that the name Jekyll derives from the French word 'je' (I) plus 'kill'. It is certainly an unusual name which is hard to forget.

✍ Writing

You have dreamed of waking up, looking into a mirror and seeing someone in it completely different to yourself, perhaps a different age, sex or race. When you look around you don't recognise the house you are in. Write a short story about what happens during your day as someone else.

H

🎭 Drama

Stevenson was fascinated by the idea of a person having both good and bad sides to their character.

A. In pairs Create a short sketch through improvisation where one person is in role as a teacher, the other as a parent. They are discussing a pupil whose behaviour at home is entirely the opposite of his behaviour at school. Role-play the pupil behaving well at home and badly at school, and vice versa.

Opening line: 'I can't believe that you are talking about my child!'

cont...

STEVENSON'S LONDON

When Stevenson wrote *The Strange Case of Dr Jekyll and Mr Hyde*, London was the wealthiest city in the world. Dr Jekyll and his friends were respectable professional men working and living in the West End, one of the richest and smartest areas of the capital.

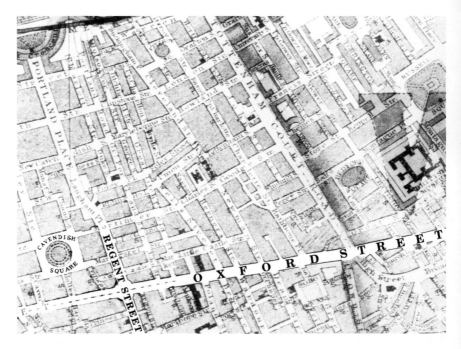

The novel tells us that Dr Lanyon lived in Cavendish Square, and we can assume that the other characters would have lived in this part of London. This area was not far from Regent Street and Oxford Street and was considered grand. The residents of such houses would have had servants to do their cooking and cleaning, to help them dress, to serve their food and open the door to callers. In the original story, both Dr Jekyll and Dr Lanyon employ butlers to manage their servants.

It is probable that many of the descriptions of London in the novel were actually inspired by Stevenson's birthplace, Edinburgh. On approaching Jekyll's house, Enfield and Utterson notice that 'The street was small … and … quiet. The inhabitants were all doing well … the street shone out in contrast to its dingy neighbourhood, like a fire in a forest; and with freshly painted shutters, well-polished brasses, and general cleanliness and gaiety of note, instantly caught and pleased the eye of the passenger.'

Not far from Cavendish Square there were very poor areas where many people would live in one room in very run-down houses, sharing outdoor toilets and water taps. Soho, one such area, was a known centre of crime and other illegal activities. In the novel, Mr Utterson visits Hyde's residence in Soho and observes 'a dingy street, a gin palace, a low French eating-house, a shop for the retail of penny numbers and two-penny salads, many ragged children in the doorways, and many women of different nationalities passing out, key in hand, to have a morning glass'.

🎭 Drama

A. In groups As can be seen from the two quotations above, Stevenson makes very obvious contrasts between the environments of the rich and poor areas of the city. How could you convey the feel of these two environments on stage? Discuss ways of creating the right atmosphere by using lighting, music and props.

B. On your own You are part of a film crew making a documentary about Stevenson's London. Draw a visual storyboard to create framed and focused pictures of the contrasts between poor and rich areas of Victorian London. Put the shots in sequence. Indicate the length and type of shot, such as a still picture, a slow-pan into the shot, a close-up or a distant shot. Add a commentary to go with the pictures on the storyboard.

C. Do **A** or **B** again, this time trying to show a view of poor and rich street life in London or a town or city you know well today. How have things changed? In what ways are they similar?

✍ Writing

In the novel, 'good' Dr Jekyll lives in smart area of London, whereas the evil Mr Hyde has rooms in a run-down, poor area. Imagine that the situations were reversed and that Hyde lived in a rich part of town, whereas Jekyll lived in a poor area. Rewrite the scene in which Hyde tramples Daisy, imagining that she was a rich girl in a 'posh' area of town. How would the reaction of the crowd have been different? Would Hyde have been able to buy his way out of the situation?

From novel to playscript

ATTACK IN THE STREET

The following extract from *The Strange Case of Dr Jekyll and Mr Hyde* describes Mr Hyde trampling a little girl. (The same scene is dramatised on pages 8–12 of the playscript.)

8–12

'I was coming home from some place at the end of the world, about three o'clock of a black winter morning, and my way led through a part of town where there was literally nothing to be seen but lamps. Street after street, and all the folks asleep – street after street, all lighted up as if for a procession, and all as empty as a church – till at last I got into that state of mind when a man listens and listens and begins to long for the sight of a policeman.

All at once, I saw two figures: one a little man who was stumping along eastward at a good walk, and the other a little girl of maybe eight or ten who was running as hard as she was able down a cross street. Well, sir, the two ran into one another naturally enough at the corner; and then came the horrible part of the thing; for the man trampled calmly over the child's body and left her screaming on the ground. It sounds nothing to hear, but it was hellish to see. It wasn't like a man; it was like some damned Juggernaut.[1] I gave a view halloa,[2] took to my heels, collared my gentleman, and brought him back to where there was already quite a group about the screaming child. He was perfectly cool and made no resistance, but he gave me one look, so ugly that it brought out the sweat on me like running. The people who had turned out were the girl's own family; and pretty soon the doctor, for whom she had been sent, put in his appearance. Well, the child was not much the worse, more frightened, according to the Sawbones;[3] and there you have supposed would be an end to it.

1. *Juggernaut* – originally this was a gigantic statue of a Hindu god which was dragged in procession at festivals. Believers were said to throw themselves under its wheels. A 'juggernaut' is a big, unstoppable moving object.
2. *View halloa* – the shout given by a huntsman when he sees a fox break cover.
3. *Sawbones* – A doctor or surgeon.

But there was one curious circumstance. I had taken a loathing to my gentleman at first sight. So had the child's family, which was only natural. But the doctor's case was what struck me. He was the usual cut-and-dry apothecary, of no particular age or colour, with a strong Edinburgh accent, and about as emotional as a bagpipe. Well, sir, he was like the rest of us: every time he looked at my prisoner, I saw that Sawbones turned sick and white with the desire to kill him. I knew what was in his mind, just as he knew what was in mine; and killing being out of the question, we did the next best.

We told the man we could and would make a scandal out of this, as should make his name stink from one end of London to the other. If he had any friends or any credit, we undertook that he should lose them.

And all the time as we were pitching it in red hot, we were keeping the women off him as best we could, for they were as wild as harpies. I never saw a circle of such hateful faces; and there was the man in the middle, with a kind of black sneering coolness – frightened too, I could see that – but carrying it off, sir, really like Satan.

"If you choose to make capital out of this accident," said he, "I am naturally helpless. No gentleman but wishes to avoid a scene," says he. "Name your figure." Well, we screwed him up to a hundred pounds for the child's family; he would dearly have liked to stick out; but there was something about the lot of us that meant mischief, and at last he struck.

The next thing was to get the money; and where do you think he carried us but to that place with the door? – whipped out a key, went in, and presently came back with the matter of ten pounds in gold and a cheque for the balance on Coutts's, drawn payable to bearer, and signed with a name that I can't mention, though it's one of the points of my story, but it was a name at least very well known and often printed. The figure was stiff; but the signature was good for more than that, if it was only genuine.

I took the liberty of pointing out to my gentleman that the whole business looked apocryphal; and that a man does not, in real life, walk into a cellar door at four in the morning and come out of it with another man's cheque for close upon a hundred pounds. But he was quite easy and sneering. "Set your mind at rest," says he; "I will stay with you until the banks open, and cash the cheque myself."

Tableau from a school production, showing Daisy being comforted after the attack by Hyde

So we all set off, the doctor, and the child's father, and our friend and myself, and passed the rest of the night in my chambers; and next day, when we had breakfasted, went in a body to the bank. I gave in the cheque myself, and said I had every reason to believe it was a forgery. Not a bit of it. The cheque was genuine.'

 **Drama**

Develop the dramatic side of the scene in which Hyde tramples the girl and experiment with the following drama forms:

A. Realism

In groups of about eight students create a still image of the moment when Enfield and the Doctor are accusing Hyde and trying to keep the crowd 'of hateful faces' away from him. The women in particular are described as 'wild as harpies'. Decide on the relationship that each person has to the others as this will dictate the attitude of that character to the girl and to Hyde. Try different methods of bringing the still image to life e.g. all shout a statement at Hyde together; shout the statement at him individually; make a comment

cont...

to another crowd member about feelings towards the event; say something to the girl or family.

Use all or some of these ideas to create a more complicated, natural and improvised version of this part of the script. Think carefully about use of space around the girl and Hyde, levels of bodies and volume of voices. Although it is supposed to look real, be aware of what an audience should see.

B. Mime – Magic Lantern – Silent Movie

Adapt the end result of **A** by taking away the words. Overaccentuate the movements and facial expressions. Experiment with slow motion, jerky moves, ordinary speed, fast speed. Maybe decide upon a mixture of different speeds to be used at different points in the scene. How do different speeds affect the end result? Try using different styles of music. How does different music affect the end result? Each member of the group could be an observer for a while to help perfect the end result. See pages 59 and 95 for music ideas.

C. Symbolism

Choose a particular moment in the scene above. Brainstorm the emotions that are felt by each character at that moment. Decide on a way in which one, some or all of these emotions might best be exaggerated. For example, you could choose one statement, such as 'You deserve to be killed' and take it in turns to say the statement in different ways by emphasising different words. You could try different variations of movements, words, and volumes until the whole group is satisfied that the emotions of the event have been dramatically produced.

D. Characterisation

Write a list of the words used in the extract to describe the way Hyde moved, looked and behaved. Choose a sentence or phrase of his speech from the novel's text. Use all this knowledge to create a version of the character with your body. This can be done individually or in twos with one person sculpting the other into body shapes and then adding the voice as in a silent movie with added soundtrack. Use the body shape, facial expression, individual mannerisms decided upon using the short piece of text and share it with others. How many different interpretations are there in the whole group? Which ones are particularly effective and why?

cont...

E. Director and playwright

Compare Stevenson's original text on pages 73–75 in these resources with the playscript adaptation on pages 8–12.

8–12

- Which words, phrases or sentences has the playwright lifted directly from the original text?

- What has been added?

- What do you think might be the reasons for these additions? The text from the novel is much longer. What sort of words are missing in the playscript?

- How can the performance of a play add these missing ideas in a different way?

Use the same scene or choose another scene and create a different version of the script which still manages to tell the story and give the right message to the audience.

✍ Writing

Write an account of Hyde trampling Daisy from Daisy's point of view, as if it was the story she told to a policeman the following day. Think about what details she might remember. Include events leading up to and after the attack. Why was she on the street in the first place?

H

Themes within and around the play

TRANSFORMATION

The writer Emma Tennant used the themes behind *Dr Jekyll and Mr Hyde* to write a modern version of the novel. She used female characters and modernised the story. In Emma Tennant's novel, Dr Frances Crane treats Mrs Hyde to help her depression and violent impulses. Mrs Hyde takes unprescribed drugs which make an interesting cocktail with the prescribed ones. She becomes younger and attractive and takes on the personality of Eliza Jekyll. The following extract is from Emma Tennant's book, *Two Women of London; The Strange Case of Ms Jekyll and Mrs Hyde*.

> I should have known. And yet – how could it be? For, close to fainting, I saw the body of the most hated, the most vilified, the most hunted woman, transform, translate itself, and, worse, for it should not be, to a form of beauty.
>
> As the stooping shoulders straightened, the neck rose straight to bear a head – still dirty, true, but appearing now simply muddied by some rustic idyll or purposely for a glossy magazine sitting – that in its confidence of beauty and arrogance literally took my breath away. And the smile! Eliza's sweet, taunting smile, which I had seen her use to such good effect on Sir James Lister and others, was beamed steadily, and totally unselfconsciously, on me.

✍ Writing

Write a short story on the theme of transformation, basing the story loosely on *Dr Jekyll and Mr Hyde*, just as Emma Tennant has done.

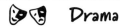 # Drama

In groups

A. Experiment with physically changing your own body shape, voice and general appearance from what you would consider to be a typical Hyde into a typical Jekyll. This could also be done with a group of you in a line, as if person one is Hyde, person two has made a subtle change, and so on, through to the final person at the end of the line who is Jekyll.

B. Add speech from the play e.g. from page 51 when Hyde changes into Jekyll in front of Lanyon:

51

HYDE Oh yes? You, who for so long denied the value of my research, you who derided your superiors – behold!

Jekyll and Hyde in the middle of the transformation (photograph from a school production of the play)

SPLIT PERSONALITY

A key theme explored by Stevenson in *Jekyll and Hyde* is the idea of the human mind being divided. These ideas foreshadowed later psychological investigations by scientists. As Jekyll says in the novel, 'I became, in my own person, a creature eaten up and emptied by fever, languidly weak both in body and mind, and solely occupied by one thought: the horror of my other self ... The powers of Hyde seemed to have grown with the sickliness of Jekyll.'

Fiction and split personality

Oscar Wilde, another famous late-19th century author, used the idea of split personality when writing his novel, *The Picture of Dorian Gray*, which was published in 1891. In it, Dorian cries, '"Each of us has Heaven and Hell in him!" ... Was it true that one could never change? He felt a wild longing for the unstained purity of his boyhood ... He knew that he had tarnished himself, filled his mind with corruption and given horror to his fancy; that he had been an evil influence to others, and had experienced a terrible joy in being so ... was there no hope for him?'

Fact and split personality

Kay Redfield Jamison wrote her personal experience of split personality in a book entitled, *An Unquiet Mind: A memoir of moods and madness.* At the age of 28 she was Assistant Professor of Psychiatry at The University of California at Los Angeles. Three months later she suffered a severe attack of manic illness (mental illness in which the sufferer can become excitable, violent or have hallucinations). She was prescribed a drug which she did not at first believe would help her, although she later realised it could save her life. This is an excerpt from her book:

In a rage I pulled the bathroom lamp off the wall and felt the
violence go through me but not out of me … I must be crazy …
I see in the mirror the blood running down my arms … I bang my
head over and over against the door … I can't stand it, I know
I'm insane again … I can't think, my life is in ruins and – worse
still – ruinous; my body is uninhabitable. It is raging and weeping
and full of destruction and wild energy gone amok. In the mirror
I see a creature I don't know but must live and share my mind with.
I understand why Jekyll killed himself before Hyde had taken over
completely. I took a massive dose of lithium with no regrets.

Lithium saved Kay Jamison's personality and she became Professor of
Psychiatry at John Hopkins University of Medicine where she
continued to research the human mind.

Discussion & Drama

A. In groups There is often a fine line between anger and madness.
Discuss with others what makes you angry. Have your emotions ever
gone too far and turned into violence or behaviour you have been
ashamed of later? What sort of everyday situation might bring out
your anger?

B. In pairs People tend to behave in different ways, depending upon who
they are with. We all take on many roles in everyday life – son or
daughter, brother or sister, grandchild, student, carer, helper,
learner, friend, best mate. Think of some everyday situations and take
on a variety of the above roles. See how the conversation and end result
changes according to your role.

C. In groups Create a role-play of a typical situation in which a young
person might find themself where anger or a mood change could be
a danger or a problem. Maybe you are taunted, bullied or put down
in front of your peers.

Brainstorm!

In groups With others, make a list of possible strategies a young
person could use to stop anger or mood changes from going too far.
Show the advice to others to see if they agree with your decisions.

DRUGS

Drugs to end a life

In *Romeo and Juliet* by William Shakespeare, Juliet accepts a drug from Friar Laurence. In Act 4, scene 1, he tells her she will not die when taking it, but describes the effects as follows:

> When presently through all thy veins shall run
> A cold and drowsy humour;[1] for no pulse
> Shall keep his native progress, but surcease;[2]
> No warmth, no breath, shall testify thou livest;
> The roses in thy lips and cheeks shall fade
> To paly ashes, thy eyes' windows[3] fall,
> Like death, when he shuts up the day of life;
> Each part, depriv'd of supple government,[4]
> Shall, stiff and stark[5] and cold, appear like death;
> And in this borrow'd likeness of shrunk death
> Thou shalt continue two and forty hours,
> And then awake as from a pleasant sleep.

1. *humour* – fluid
2. *no pulse… but surcease* – the natural rhythm of the pulse will stop
3. *eyes' windows* – eyelids
4. *supple government* – the control that makes it move and bend
5. *stark* – rigid

Juliet's tomb at Verona

In Act 5, scene 1, Romeo wrongly thinks Juliet is dead. He visits an apothecary to buy poison to commit suicide.

APOTHECARY	Who calls so loud?
ROMEO	Come hither, man. I see that thou art poor.
	Hold, There is forty ducats;[1] let me have
	A dram[2] of poison, such soon-speeding gear[3]
	As will disperse itself through all the veins
	That the life-weary taker may fall dead,
	And that the trunk may be discharg'd of breath
	As violently as hasty powder fir'd
	Doth hurry from the fatal cannon's womb.
APOTHECARY	Such mortal drugs I have; but Mantua's law
	Is death to any he that utters[4] them.
ROMEO	Art thou so bare and full of wretchedness
	And fear'st to die? Famine is in thy cheeks,
	Need and oppression starveth in thine eyes,[5]
	Contempt and beggary hang upon thy back;
	The world is not thy friend nor the world's law;
	The world affords[6] no law to make thee rich:
	Then be not poor, but break it and take this.[7]
APOTHECARY	My poverty but not my will consents.
ROMEO	I pay thy poverty and not thy will.
APOTHECARY	Put this in any liquid thing[8] you will,
	And drink it off; and if you had the strength
	Of twenty men, it would dispatch you straight.
ROMEO	There is thy gold – worse poison to men's souls,
	Doing more murder in this loathsome world
	Than these poor compounds that thou mayst not sell.
	I sell thee poison: thou hast sold me none.
	Farewell; buy food and get thyself in flesh.[9]
	Come, cordial and not poison, go with me
	To Juliet's grave; for there must I use thee.

1. *A ducat* was a gold coin. Forty ducats was a large sum of money.
2. *soon-speeding gear* – quickly working substance.
3. *dram* – glass.
4. *utters* – sells.
5. *Need ... eyes* – It can be seen from your eyes that want and oppression are killing you.
6. *affords* – provides.
7. *break it and take this* – break the law and take this money.
8. *Put this in any liquid thing* – Romeo does not do this. He drinks it undiluted.
9. *Set thyself in flesh* – two meanings: grow fatter, or get leather or sheepskin clothing.

Romeo uses abusive and persuasive language as well as bribery to obtain the drug. He is prepared to risk the taking of a liquid knowing nothing of its contents or the result it may well have upon his body.

✍ Writing

Notice that the lines from *Romeo and Juliet* are written in verse with five beats and ten syllables on each line (pentameters).

A. Read Robert Louis Stevenson's description of the effects of the drug upon Jekyll as he changed into Hyde:

———————————

The most racking pains succeeded: a grinding in the bones, deadly nausea, and a horror of the spirit that cannot be exceeded at the hour of birth or death. Then these agonies began swiftly to subside, and I came to myself as if out of a great sickness. There was something strange in my sensations, something indescribably new and, from its novelty, incredibly sweet. I felt younger, lighter, happier in body; within I was conscious of a heady recklessness, a current of disordered sensual images running like a mill race in my fancy, a solution of the bonds of obligation, an unknown but not an innocent freedom of the soul. I knew myself, at the first breath of this new life, to be more wicked, tenfold more wicked, sold a slave to my original evil; and the thought, in that moment, braced and delighted me like wine. I stretched out my hands, exulting in the freshness of these sensations; and in the act, I was suddenly aware that I had lost in stature.

———————————

Working alone or with others, use Stevenson's words with ideas of your own and try turning them into verse which has ten syllables on each line for example:

'The most racking pangs of agony came.
Grinding in my bones, dry, screaming, aching.'

cont...

B. Use the idea of opposites – before and after transformation, good and evil – to create poetry in any style. *Ideas:*

- Alternate one line good and one line evil;

- Alternate verses of one good and one evil;

- Use visual line patterns to create a good side of a page and an evil side; gradually increase the lines in length, as if the evil words are taking over from the good.

C. Use the *Romeo and Juliet* text or poetry you have written around the theme of *Jekyll and Hyde* and present it to others in a creative way. Use live or recorded music suitable to the atmosphere, sound effects, layers of voice and sound, and movement to present poetry as performance. (See page 92 for music suggestions.)

Illegal drugs and youth

Look at the pictures below and on page 86. The images on page 86 represent substances that are commonly abused. The quotation describes the effects of such abuse on Sid Vicious, a member of the band The Sex Pistols.

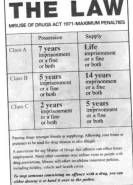

Sid was naive but full of wit about things. Excellent person, but drugs did him in and turned him into a deeply unpleasant Mr Hyde – one who would make us "hyde" from him at times. It's not nice to be with someone talking ga-ga and gibberish and being belligerent about his own hangovers and hang-ups. There's a terrible incoherence that comes in with drugs. Any kind of addiction is self-torture and slow suicide.

(*Rotten: No Irish, No Dogs, No Blacks – The Authorised Autobiography of Johnny Rotten of the Sex Pistols* (1993), by Johny Lydon with Keith and Kent Zimmerman)

Writing/Discussion

A. On your own The quotation on page 86 is written by Johnny Rotten (John Lydon) about his friend, Sid Vicious. What might a friend of Jekyll, like Lanyon or Utterson, have written about the change in Jekyll in an account given to a reporter or police officer?

B. Imagine you are a Victorian reporter at the time of either the trampling of the girl or the murder of Carew. Write a newspaper article with a striking headline. Include interviews with eyewitnesses. If you are doing a live performance of the play the copies of the story could be laid out using desktop publishing, then distributed by the newsboys to the audience (see pages 21 and 25 of the playscript).

C. Write a newspaper article that outlines the final scene of the play. There are so many questions hanging in the air. Where is Hyde? How did Jekyll die? What will an autopsy of the body discover? Utterson has the will. Does he tell the press all he knows?

D. As a class Set up a debate discussing topical drugs issues. You could use one of the motions below, or think up your own.

- This house believes that educating young people about the dangers of drugs is the only way forward.

- This house believes that our drugs laws need to be changed.

- This house believes that there should be harsher penalties for drug abusers.

Prescribed drugs and youth

The following discussion was heard on various US radio stations. It was based around the idea that anti-depressants prescribed for children with learning difficulties, or Attention Deficit Disorder, might be linked to high school shootings in the USA. This is a call which came in to the radio programme:

MARY: Hi, I have ADD (Attention Deficit Disorder) and I took Prozac for about four months. I stopped because I didn't notice it was doing anything. I started taking Welbutrin, because the doctors said, "You need this," and I am seventeen and I figured that this would be better for me. I missed the doses and my body was freaking out because I was used to this stuff … I started noticing patterns of anger … I would get up in the morning and I wouldn't want to get out of bed. I can see why all those kids did that stuff like kill people because it makes you angry … I am not surprised people are committing suicide. I freaked out for two days, screaming at my mom. I'm not on it any more and I'm glad because it screwed up everything … there are other ways besides drugs …

DR. PETER BREGEN: I'm so sorry that my profession of medicine does this to our nation's young … The drugs have changed your brain just like alcohol. You shouldn't abruptly stop taking these drugs …

JEFF RENSE (PRESENTER): Here is a young woman feeling she has a learning disorder … and she's listening to this programme – which is a wonderful forum for information. She obviously has a desire to expand her mind.

DR. PETER BREGEN: There's nothing wrong with your brain. The answer is not to think you have to tinker with your brain. I wouldn't turn to mind-altering substances. Maybe counselling if you are troubled about the direction of your life …

(Source: 'Prescribed drugs can harm your health' – from the 'Sightings'
programme on Talk Radio (103.7FM), Arkansas, USA.
Taken from a written article in *The Guardian Editor*.

---

෫෫ ෫෫ Discussion

In groups It is hard for a young person to make important decisions about their life, particularly if they are unwell or unhappy. It is normal to ask for advice from adults. Sometimes adults give opposing opinions and different advice. Talk with your friends about any situations that you know have been confusing for you – situations where you have been given mixed messages and have had difficulty making decisions. Have the problems changed much over the past century? Do you think that the youth of the 1890s experienced similar problems?

Writing

A. In pairs The radio programme excerpt is a transcript (written copy) of what was said. What features of the writing tell us that these words were spoken rather than written?

B. On your own Use the transcript to write an article for a youth magazine. Change the language so that it is in the third person (e.g. *he said, she said, the discussion was about...*) but make it suitable for an audience of young people. What photos would you like to include? What will the captions underneath be? How will you title the report?

H

New drugs – their creation and their use

Role-play

As a class The teacher, in role as a well-known scientist, invites students (in role as respected experts in the fields of criminology, medicine, sociology, theology, psychology etc.) to attend a one-day top secret conference to debate the use of a new drug. Each student must swear on oath never to repeat anything that is discussed during the conference.

Scientists have developed a drug that changes the personality of the person who takes it, so that they become well-adjusted human beings who never do wrong. The experts debate whether the drug should be used as a way of stopping criminal activity. Should a dose of it be given to children who misbehave, or to prisoners?

Debate
The experts discuss the situation in small groups holding the views relevant to their occupation. They return to the full conference to share ideas aloud to others.

Sociogram of opinions in role as experts
A bottle containing the drug is placed in the middle of the space. The experts are asked to express their support for the use of the drug by standing close to the bottle if they think it is an excellent idea, in the middle of the space if they are unsure, and against the wall if they definitely consider the drug to be a bad idea. Count and discuss the result.

cont...

Conscience alley

Students make an alley of bodies facing each other. The teacher or a student in role as the developer of the wonder drug walks through the two lines of conference participants. Each participant makes a statement to or asks a question of the developer reflecting their opinion of his/her creation. For example: Do you have the right to control another human being's actions? What if the dosage is given incorrectly? Do you really know about the after-effects? If everyone was perfect there would be no variety in life.

Final secret ballot

Each conference member is given a ballot paper and asked to tick if they consider the drug should be legally used or put a cross if they do not want it to be used. Discuss the final results.

✍ Writing

H

On your own Write a magazine article on the first trials of the new drug, including comments from experts in a different field.

Top secret conference and the media

NEW MOVES TO TACKLE CRIMINAL ADDICTS

Home Office Minister George Howarth has called for new powers following the release of a Government study on the links between drugs and crime.

Figures reveal that six out of ten criminals arrested test positive for drugs and that addicts were responsible for stealing £2.5 billion worth of property last year.

Inspector Hill added, "Drugs are a major cause of crime and it's probably safe to say that the majority of burglaries in this year were drug-related. I'd therefore back any plans to tackle the problem and certainly the introduction of counselling and treatment programmes would be of great benefit."

Inspector May said, "While I'd welcome the introduction of treatment enforcement, I still think there are a few hard-core addicts who simply don't want any help."

(Adapted from *Dorset Evening Echo*)

✍ Writing

Read the above newspaper article. Use the same headline to write an article which describes the use of the new wonder drug introduced at the Top Secret Conference on page 89. The new drug is to be part of the counselling and treatment programme. Who will be interviewed? What do the police/local people/criminals and their relatives think of the idea?

H

🎭 Drama

A. In pairs Role-play TV interviews between any of the characters from the Top Secret Conference or the newspaper article.

B. In groups Create the drama which happens at the home of one of the criminals who has been found guilty of theft. He/she needs money for drugs and is now going to be given the wonder drug to make him/her behave perfectly.

C. In groups Create the drama in the cell where the criminal is told by the prison medical staff that they are to be given a wonder drug that will stop them from breaking the law.

Drugs and young people

ROCK STAR COMMENTS

"I urge all youngsters to educate themselves about the harmful side of drug taking. I've said it before and I'll say it again, the best policy is, don't start."

(Noel Gallagher of Oasis in interview.)

(The Guardian)

A MOTHER SPEAKS OUT

Our middle son began experimenting with drugs more than 10 years ago when he was 15. It manifested itself in a typical way: his school work deteriorated and he lost interest in sporting activities, his only friends became those similarly experimenting and his need for money quickly involved him in trouble with the police. His personality changed almost overnight from a loving, easy-going and unselfish child to a defiantly aggressive teenager. After 10 years of drug abuse he became more and more paranoid and panic stricken ... talking incessantly about the voices he could hear in his head. He was taken to a secure psychiatric hospital. Skilled and sympathetic staff told us that he was suffering from a drug-induced psychosis, a schizophrenic-type illness from which he might or might not recover.

(The Guardian)

BRITISH CRIME SURVEY

Almost one in six young people take illegal drugs on a regular basis, according to government figures released today. The findings, part of the British Crime Survey, show that cannabis is most commonly used.

**People who have ever taken drugs: by type of drug and age
England and Wales**   **Percentages**

	16–19	20–24	25–34	35–44	45–59	All ages 16–59
Cannabis	35	42	30	23	8	22
Amphetamines	16	21	11	7	3	9
LSD	10	15	6	4	1	5
Magic mushrooms	7	12	8	4	1	5
Ectasy	9	13	4	1	1	3
Cocaine	2	6	4	3	1	3
Solvents	5	7	3	1	–	2
Crack	1	2	1	1	–	1
Heroin	1	1	1	1	–	1
Any drug	45	49	37	29	13	29

Source: British Crime Survey, Home Office

(The Guardian)

DRUGS CULTURE DOES NOT EXIST

Yesterday's report concluded 'that most young people who use illicit drugs are sociable, sensible and have strong ties of trust and respect with their families. Contrary to the public image, they are not reckless, alienated losers, lacking self-esteem and unable to resist peer pressure. The researchers found them less introverted than those who do not use drugs, leading active lives in which drug taking was an integrated part of certain social events.'

(The Guardian)

⬤⬤ Discussion

In groups Read all the extracts on pages 91–93 and discuss the contents. There are opposing views.

- What do you think about the use of drugs for leisure, drugs for escape, drugs as a way of becoming one of the crowd?
- What are the dangers?
- Why do people take drugs at all?

Writing

Look closely at the survey results on page 92. Write a list of questions which you think would need to be asked to obtain these results. Having written your survey try it out on a variety of people of different ages. Are there any problems you are likely to encounter? Can you avoid these before you start?

H

GENETIC ENGINEERING

Jekyll, as a scientist, was testing barriers, experimenting with not only drugs but also his own mind, behaviour and body. Many scientists today are experimenting in a variety of ways to improve the human situation. Could there be dangers like those Jekyll faced?

Genetic Weapons to Provide Force for High-tech Ethnic War

by Jeremy Laurance, Health Editor

Genetic weapons that could be targeted at specific racial groups in a form of hi-tech ethnic warfare are to be investigated by the British Medical Association.

They do not exist but could be available in five to ten years, the association said. Doctors fear developments in genetic therapy to cure disease might be turned to evil ends in the hands of a dictator.

Scientists expect to be able to produce the first genetically targeted drugs in five years. The drugs would repair faulty DNA within the cell and might be used to treat conditions such as diabetes and cystic fibrosis. Dr Nathanson, head of science and ethics at BMA, said: 'No one has been able to tell us why, if we can produce genetically targeted drugs with a good effect, we won't be able to produce similar drugs with a bad effect in the same time-scale.'

The Human Genome Project, which is mapping the entire human genetic code, might produce enough information to allow specific genetic types to be identified. 'We know the genes for hair colour, eye colour and height. If 90 per cent of the enemy have blue eyes, blond hair and are over six feet tall, that could be the cluster you are looking for.' Certain blood types were commoner in different ethnic groups and could also be targeted, Dr Nathanson said.

(The Independent)

⟨⟩ ⟨⟩ Discussion

As a class Brainstorm the good and bad sides of genetically targeted drugs. What are the possible dangers for human beings and possible advantages for the future health of the world?

Debate: *This house believes that genetic drugs are safe.*

😮😊 Drama

In groups You are the TV news team that has to investigate good and bad sides of genetically targeted drugs. You must convey to the people watching the news all aspects of the story. Create interview situations with relevant characters, for instance a famous genetic scientist, a young person who has diabetes or cystic fibrosis, Dr Nathanson or members of the public.

✍ Research and Writing

In groups or on your own Collect any articles, food labels or advertisements from magazines and newspapers which mention genetic engineering. Make a scrap-book with notes under the different items explaining where they come from. Write an introduction to the book outlining the main issues.

H

Research resources and further reading

Other genres, versions and interpretations of the storyline of *The Strange Case of Dr Jekyll and Mr Hyde*.

Books include:
The Picture of Dorian Gray by Oscar Wilde, Penguin, 1994
Jekyll, Alias Hyde by Donald Thomas, Papermac, 1989
Two women of London: The Strange Case of Ms Jekyll and Mrs Hyde by Emma Tennant, Faber, 1990
Mary Reilly by Valerie Martin, Black Swan, 1991
Dr Jekyll and Mr Hyde retold by John Grant, an 'Usborne Library of Fear, Fantasy and Adventure' adaptation, Usborne, 1995
Jacqueline Hyde by Robert Swindells, Doubleday, 1996

Movies include:
Dr Jekyll and Mr Hyde, starring John Barrymore, 1921
Doctor Jekyll and Mr Hyde, starring Fredric March, 1931
Dr Jekyll and Mr Hyde, starring Spencer Tracy, 1941
Son of Dr Jekyll, 1951
The Two Faces of Dr Jekyll, 1960
The Nutty Professor, a comedy starring Jerry Lewis, 1963
I, Monster, starring Christopher Lee, 1971
The Strange Case of Dr Jekyll and Miss Osbourne, 1983
The Jekyll Experiment, 1986
Dr Jekyll and Mr Hyde, Australian animated TV movie, 1988
Edge of Sanity, 1988
Jekyll and Hyde, 1995
Dr Jekyll and Ms Hyde, 1995
The Nutty Professor, starring Eddie Murphy, 1996
Mary Reilly, starring Julia Roberts and John Malkovich, 1996

Music Resources:
Twin Peaks – by Angelo Badalamenti, Warner Brothers
Horror! Monsters, Witches and Vampires, Silva Treasury SILVAD 3507X
Thrillers, Silva Treasury

Trainspotting 1, various artists, EMI Premier 7243 8 37190 2 0
Trainspotting 2, various artists, EMI Soundtracks 7243 8 21265 2 2
(explicit lyrics warning)
Carrington by Michael Nyman, Argo 444 873 2 ZHJ
The Draughtsman's Contract by Michael Nyman, CASCD1158 0777 7
86463 2 7 R
Romeo and Juliet, various artists, EMI Soundtracks 7243 8 59871 2 0

Dance Resources:

There is a very good BBC Dance Education Series, which was televised
for schools to record in 1998, called *Dance TV*. It is also available to
purchase with teachers' notes. The local Dance Advisor/Inspector may
well have made a copy. There are five 30-minute programmes – 'Dance
Athletes', 'Street Dance', 'Dance Rhythms', 'Partner Dance' and
'Teaching Today: Dance'. Programme 2: Street Dance includes some
good ideas and includes an excerpt from the dance, 'Blue Flowers' in
which street dancer Banksy dances in a trio, portraying the idea of
Victorian body snatchers. The choreography is a good starting point or
inspiration for the themes behind *Dr Jekyll and Mr Hyde*. There is also a
video available from BBC Education Information Services on 0181 746
1111, or view their website http://www.bbc.co.uk/education.